WOODROW POLSTON

ENEMY OF THE SAINTS
THE RISE OF ANTICHRIST

POLSTON HOUSE
PUBLISHING

Enemy of the Saints
Copyright © 2016 by Woodrow Polston. All rights reserved.

No part of this publication may be reproduced, stored in a retrieval system or transmitted in any way by any means, electronic, mechanical, photocopy, recording or otherwise without the prior permission of the author except as provided by USA copyright law.

This book is designed to provide accurate and authoritative information with regard to the subject matter covered. This information is given with the understanding that neither the author nor Polston House Publishing, LLC is engaged in rendering legal, professional advice.

The opinions expressed by the author are not necessarily those of Polston House Publishing, LLC.

Published by Polston House Publishing LLC
www.PolstonHouse.com

Book design copyright © 2016 by Polston House Publishing, LLC. All rights reserved.

Published in the United States of America

ISBN-13: 978-0692857205
ISBN-10: 0692857206

Religion / Biblical Commentary/

Bible Prophecy

Contents

Introduction 9

1 What We Know About the Antichrist 13

   The God of His Fathers 14
   The Beast and Babylon 17
   The Supernatural Mystery 22
   His Picture Develops 25

2 Who Will Support Him and Why 29

   The Rise of an Immoral Culture 30
   A Godless Society 34
   World Greed and World Power 39

3 The World Falls Apart to Fall into Place 43

   The Destabilization of the Mind 44
   The Increase of Sorcery 47
   Scenarios of Natural Disasters 49
   A Massive Loss of Life 53

4 The Mark of the Beast 59

   The Mystery of the Mark 60
   The Shepherd of Lost Souls 64
   To Depend on God or Government 68

5	Technology to Control the Masses	73
	Microchips and Satellites	74
	Scalar Weapons and Weather Modification	77
	A Call for Global Government	82
	At the Touch of a Button	89
6	The Manifestation of Demons on Earth	93
	Signs of Their Coming	94
	When the Pit Opens Up	97
	The Return of the Fallen Angels	101
	The Greatest Horror on Earth	110
7	What Will Become of the Church?	117
	To Be Closed Or Converted?	117
	The Congregation Become the Ministers	121
	Apocalyptic Survival	123
8	A Nightmare Becomes Reality	133
	Prophetic Dreams	134
	When People Eat Their Own	144
	Death Is Desired, and Death Is Not Found	149
9	After the Rapture	153
	When Will It Occur?	154
	Who Will Be Left?	160
	The Prize of the Overcomer	161

10	Of Death and Damnation	165
	Detention Centers and Death Camps	166
	The Point of No Return	178
	Life Goes On, but Not for Long	180
11	Hell Lies Waiting	183
	The Atmosphere of Hell	184
	Subterranean Cities	190
	Darkness and Eternal Torment	195
12	When Our Leaders Become Lawless	197
	Leaders in the Church	197
	Leaders of the Nation	199
	The Vision of Judgment	202
13	Righteousness Prevails	207
	The War on Christianity	208
	The Banishment of Evil	214
	King of Kings, Lord of lords	217
	Eternal Life, Eternal Light	218
Notes		221

Introduction

There is no escaping it, no preventing it—the hellish reality that is destined to be the end result for all humanity and life as we know it on earth. Who is he that was spoken of old, destined to be the final ruler before the return of Christ? What will the world look like under his reign? Is it possible that he is alive today, walking among us unknown until he receives his power and authority?

As we continue to soar in the realm of technology, we inch ourselves ever closer to a world that could be completely controlled by an evil government. Are we seeing the natural progression of creativity, or have we been given tools and enlightenment from spirits and fallen angels that will make possible the implementation of an evil one world order? If the last state of the world is to be controlled by an evil government and ultimately a leader who is possessed with the power of Satan himself, there is no doubt that evil forces are at work in world policies today.

If we consider the clues given to us in the scriptures concerning the Antichrist, we can determine certain conclusions regarding his identity. Why will he be so widely accepted if he is going to be the most brutal dictator that the world has ever seen? How do current cultures and world affairs prove to be the right environment for the rise of such a leader? Will we know him when we see him?

Is it likely that we who are now living have front row tickets to see the greatest horror ever played out on the earth? Or do we only assume that the end is near, just as our ancestors believed that they would see the end? We know that in order for a one world government to control us, there must first be a world government. Before this can happen, our current systems must be broken down so that a new order can be introduced.

With the global economy in distress, we can see how things are quickly breaking down. That is perhaps one of the most significant signs we have that none of our ancestors did. With the uncertainty of the economy, the decline in moral values, the loss of common sense in politics, and the decline of interest in scriptural knowledge, we can begin to understand how the masses become sheep. And all the sheep will follow without question, even to the slaughter.

Let us review what we know and perhaps some things that have been overlooked about the beast that is destined to control the world. Also, let us consider what nightmares we may face, as we are surrounded by an evil society and oppressed under an evil rule. The important thing to keep in mind here is to know that you are saved by Jesus Christ. And if like me you are willing to die for what you believe in rather than selling your soul for the sake of your life, we really have nothing to fear.

> And it was given unto him to make war
> with the saints, and to overcome them:
> and power was given him over all
> kindreds, and tongues, and nations.
> (Revelation 13:7)

1

What We Know About the Antichrist

If you were to ask the question, "Who is the Antichrist?" almost anyone can tell you that he is the prophesied world leader of the end times. But is there deeper insight? How close can we get to the true identity of the one who will destroy the saints of God? If we break down key verses in scripture, we can develop a clear picture of who he is and how he fits into modern society.

If you were to search the Internet for a line up of suspects, you would find many candidates that are accused of being the Antichrist. It seems that every new president that is elected is automatically a prime suspect, even dating back to Ronald Wilson Reagan. He was a prime suspect due to his full name equaling the number 666. However, as easy as it is to believe any of our recent presidents could be the one, it has thus far been impossible, due to certain clues from the scriptures about his characteristics.

So let us look at the details that will quickly rule out the accused, narrow down the suspects, and possibly shed light on the otherwise unsuspected. Whether he be alive and among us today, or many years into the future, a study such as this will surely help us to better identify him with more certainty. While we will surely know him when he begins his reign, prior knowledge will certainly help us to prepare, and to also warn others.

First we will study what we know about his religious affiliation, possible religious background, and how he will ultimately make a god of himself and be worshiped by all those whose names are not written in the book of life. There are multiple scenarios that could unfold regarding the aspect of the religious atmosphere during his initial rise to power. If we consider all the possibilities and keep them in mind, we can closely watch for signs of their development.

The God of His Fathers

In the book of Daniel, we find very interesting clues regarding the religious stance of the Antichrist. The following verse tells us numerous things regarding the religious background of his ancestry.

> Neither shall he regard the God of
> his fathers, nor the desire of women,
> nor regard any god: for he shall
> magnify himself above all.
> (Daniel 11:37)

Considering God is capitalized in this verse, we can say with certainty that this verse is describing the only true God, the God of Abraham, Isaac, and Jacob. Therefore, this tells us that the ancestors of the Antichrist did in fact worship our God. So what can we learn from this clue regarding his identity? If he is a descendant of Jews or Christians, then where would he most likely be found geographically? Would the most likely location be Europe or the United States of America? While it is possible that he would be in the Middle East and of Arab descent, it is less likely due to other factors which we shall cover in later sections of the study.

Let us look at some other verses of interest concerning God and a mystery god which his fathers knew not and what they might disclose regarding the geographical location of his origin and what cultural background would be the most likely environment to produce him.

> But in his estate shall he honour the
> God of forces: and a god whom his
> fathers knew not shall he honour
> with gold, and silver, and with
> precious stones, and pleasant things.
> (Daniel 11:38)

Again as in the last verse, we see God capitalized. After that, we see a god acknowledged in lowercase. This would strongly suggest that he is in a nation that has a large Christian or Jewish population. If he does not regard

God, then he would only initially honor Him for the sake of political acceptance in his estate. But who is the god mentioned whom his fathers knew not?

Could it be that a new god will evolve and become world renown in the time of the end? Or is the god mentioned in this verse already here? One scenario would be that if he were in Europe or the United States, he would have to initially acknowledge God, and possibly Allah as well. If this were the case, the verse would be suggesting that he would pay honor to God and pay a higher honor to Allah. Let us take a look at the next verse for further details.

> Thus shall he do in the most strong holds with a strange god, whom he shall acknowledge and increase with glory: and he shall cause them to rule over many, and shall divide the land for gain.
> (Daniel 11:39)

If he is honoring this strange god in the strong holds and this strange god is Allah, this would suggest that he is seeking support from the Muslim people, and ultimately the Middle East. For him to cause people to come under rule of this strange god, this obviously suggests that religious freedom in the western world has been lost. We can say with certainty that if he comes from the western world, his fathers did not know Allah.

The Beast and Babylon

Just as debated as the identity of the Antichrist is the question of where mystery Babylon is located. Considering the fact that the city of Babylon mentioned in the Old Testament is a desolate place, which is located in modern-day Iraq, it is impossible to be mystery Babylon. There would be no mystery about it if it were. Mystery Babylon is described in the book of Revelation as a major market in the world at the time of the end. It would take trillions of dollars and many decades if not centuries to build up the Babylon of Iraq for such a world status.

There are interesting connections to be made between verses from Isaiah, Jeremiah, Daniel, and Revelation—all regarding Babylon and the possibility that the Antichrist rises to power and begins his reign there. There are also significant clues that would suggest that this mystery Babylon is likely the United States. Let us first look at the verses that would suggest that Babylon might be America.

> Behold, I will stir up the Medes against
> them, which shall not regard silver; and
> as for gold, they shall not delight in it.
> (Isaiah 13:17)

This verse implies that Babylon will be attacked, and yet there will be no interest in taking booty. This would suggest an attack from an enemy that is only interested in the destruction of the inhabitants due to hatred and indifference. As we are well aware, there are many in the Middle East that despise the American people and our way of life. There is a call from the Muslim extremists for a jihad on America more and more often as time goes on. If there were an incident such as a natural disaster, which would temporarily cripple us, a nation such as Iran with the help of Russia could likely destroy us in one day.

> It shall never be inhabited, neither shall it be dwelt in from generation to generation: neither shall the Arabian pitch tent there; neither shall the shepherds make their fold there. (Isaiah 13:20)

This verse tells us that the land will be made desolate and the invading army will not use the land for building or inhabiting. This could also rule out the possibility of Babylon being located in the Middle East. If the Arabian will not pitch tent there, this could suggest that Arab armies have invaded a nation that has little Arab population. To say that they would not pitch tent there strongly implies that this location is not in the Middle East because the Arab people have always lived there.

> A sword is upon their horses, and
> upon their chariots, and upon all the

> mingled people that are in the midst
> of her. (Jeremiah 50:37)
> We would have healed Babylon,
> but she is not healed: forsake her,
> and let us go every one into his own
> country: for her judgment reacheth
> unto heaven, and is lifted up even
> to the skies. (Jeremiah 51:9)

These verses indicate a location that has diverse cultures, mingled peoples, and a multitude of citizens from numerous countries. This would only add to the possibilities of the United States being mystery Babylon. Is there any nation on earth so diverse in culture, national background, and such a mix of mingled people? And at the same time one that is abundant in treasures and sitting on many waters?

> O thou that dwellest upon many waters,
> abundant in treasures, thine end is come,
> and the measure of thy covetousness.
> (Jeremiah 51:13)

Now let us look at some of the verses that would suggest that the Antichrist rises to power in Babylon. What are the connections between this mystery Babylon and the empire of the Antichrist? Does he come to his demise at the time of the destruction of mystery Babylon? If not, will he continue to rule and wreak havoc from another location after it is laid to waste?

The Destruction of Babylon

For out of the north there cometh up a nation against her, which shall make her land desolate, and none shall dwell therein: they shall remove, they shall depart, both man and beast. (Jeremiah 50:3)

For, lo, I will raise and cause to come up against Babylon an assembly of great nations from the north country: and they shall set themselves in array against her; from thence she shall be taken: their arrows shall be as of a mighty expert man; none shall return in vain. (Jeremiah 50:9)

The Empire of the Antichrist

And at the time of the end shall the king of the south push at him: and the king of the north shall come against him like a whirlwind, with chariots, and with horsemen, and with many ships; and he shall enter into the countries, and shall overflow and pass over. (Daniel 11:40)

With these verses concerning Babylon and the empire of the Antichrist, we see the similarity of sudden destruction. Both locations are made desolate by a great army which comes from the north. In the description regarding the Antichrist, we see that he escapes this attack and enters into other countries. If we continue to read the following verses, we learn that he enters into the glorious land and eventually plants the tabernacles of his palace between the seas in the glorious holy mountain. And this is described to be just prior to his end.

Finally, let us attempt to connect the verses that describe Satan, the beast, and Babylon, all as John saw them. A close look reveals that their description is nearly identical.

The Description of Satan

> And there appeared another wonder in heaven; and behold a great red dragon, having seven heads and ten horns, and Seven crowns upon his heads.
> (Revelation 12:3)

The Description of the Beast

> And I stood upon the sand of the sea, and saw a beast rise up out of the sea, having seven heads and ten horns, and upon his horns ten crowns, and upon his heads the names of blasphemy.
> (Revelation 13:1)

The only difference between the great red dragon, who is Satan, and the beast is that the dragon has only seven crowns upon his seven heads where the beast has ten crowns upon his ten horns.

The Description of Babylon

So he carried me away in the spirit into the wilderness: and I saw a woman sit upon a scarlet colored beast, full of names of blasphemy, having seven heads and ten horns. (Revelation 17:3)

In the description of mystery Babylon, we read of a scarlet- colored beast, and in the description of Satan, we read of a great red dragon—two descriptions of a red-colored beast. And again, we see the same description of the beast having seven heads and ten horns, full of names of blasphemy.

The Supernatural Mystery

There are many instances in the scriptures that involve a supernatural aspect of the Antichrist. Is he a man who is born naturally, just as any other? Or has he already lived in a previous time, waiting in a dark place, reserved for the time of the end? Our questions are posed from the cryptic writings of John, in the book of Revelation, where he speaks of a beast with a deadly wound that was healed. A beast that was, and is not, and yet is.

> The beast that thou sawest was, and is not; and shall ascend out of the bottomless pit, and go into perdition: and they that dwell on the earth shall wonder, whose names were not written in the book of life from the foundation of the world, when they behold the beast that was, and is not, and yet is. (Revelation 17:8)

If we are to consider this beast to be a kingdom, which was, and is not, and yet is, it would seem to make sense that the original Babylonian empire would rise again. Though as I stated previously, it would be trillions of dollars and decades into the future if so. If it were a world kingdom, it also fits the trend of the evil counterfeits of Satan. It would be the evil version of the new Jerusalem coming down from heaven, because it is described as coming up from the bottomless pit. And as we know, just as there is the holy trinity, there is an unholy trinity, comprised of Satan, the Antichrist, and the false prophet.

However, continuing to read into the following verses, we discover that the seven heads are identified as seven mountains. And there are seven kings, five which are fallen, one that is, and the other has not yet come. And the beast that was, and is not, even he is the eighth, and is of the seven. So here we have the description of a king, who was, and is not, and yet is to come. These verses, Revelation

17:10–11, tells us possibly more than any others regarding the beast.

We have here the clear description of a man because he is described as a king, not a kingdom or mountain or head or horn or crown. Considering this information, the nature of the Antichrist only becomes more and more of a mystery. Because now we not only have a man who will mysteriously rise to rule the world, but it would seem as though he was once dead and somehow is resurrected. Could another possibility be that he was at one time living on earth and was taken down to the pit and reserved for the last days? We know that there are two instances in the Bible where mortal men have been taken up to heaven by God and reserved to come back as the two witnesses in the last days. These two men, Elijah and Enoch, have never died. So could there be a counterfeit taken down to the pit in the same fashion?

In either case, whether it be resurrection or supernatural preservation, it is almost too much to comprehend. We have, however, established a strong connection between mystery Babylon and the Antichrist. Babylon is a nation or world power, which he is a king of, and the power of the kingdom is received from the great red dragon, who is identified as Satan in Revelation 12:9.

Let us now review in detail all the characteristics that make up the beast, from the clues given to us in the scriptures, and how they relate to our modern day society.

With everything that is going on in the world, it is now easier than ever for us who study prophecy to discern certain details. And it is now more likely than ever for such a leader to rise to power, and to deceive the masses.

His Picture Develops

Possibly the most telling piece of prophetic insight concerning the Antichrist is found in the book of Daniel. We read about the rise of a vile person, who is not given the honor of the kingdom. And yet he obtains it peaceably, by his flatteries. We are also informed that he will be diverse from his fathers and shall rule unlike any before him. The best clue to his identity is the fact that he will not regard the desire of women. This would either suggest that he is a homosexual or that he simply is not wasting his time with a sexual relationship.

> *He will not regard the desire of women.*
> Neither shall he regard the God of his fathers,
> nor the desire of women, nor regard any god:
> For he shall magnify himself above all.
> (Daniel 11:37)

With this key piece of information, we can eliminate all the presidents who have been among the accused in the last few decades. If the Antichrist in fact has a wife, it would only be a marriage of opportunity. Only for the sake of the public eye, but even then it should be obvious if he were a homosexual. There almost certainly would not be children involved, and if there were, they would not be his, and we would know that.

He is a vile person and loves to flatter.

> And in his estate shall stand up a vile person, to whom they shall not give the honour of the kingdom: but he shall come in peaceably, and obtain the kingdom by flatteries.
> (Daniel 11:21)

In Daniel's vision, could he have seen evidence that the Antichrist is a homosexual, therefore labeling him a vile person? Or did Daniel see in his vision women advancing themselves at him, that he quickly turned down? It would have to be one or the other for him to say that he does not regard the desire of women, would it not? One thing that is clear is that he is a master of flattery. If he is capable of obtaining a kingdom by wooing the people with words, we should certainly watch closely all those who say all the right things.

Many leaders in the past have proven to be good examples of this, winning the people with optimistic speech and false hope. Perhaps the best example of this was Adolf Hitler. Who rallied the masses and soon after slaughtered countless people. A more subtle example would be the election of Barrack Obama, who won the people with words and did little more than simply that.

He will make a god of himself.

And all that dwell upon the earth shall
worship him, whose names are not
written in the book of life of the Lamb
slain from the foundation of the world.
(Revelation 13:8)

Before he receives his kingdom and his power, this verse tells us clues that will be detectable at an early stage. A selfish person, obsessed with himself, and only concerned with self-pleasure and glory—a character trait emerges that is shared with homosexuality. Gay people are always about self-pleasure; it is more than a sexual preference, but it is an all -the-time consuming way of life, all about themselves. This would also make him an enemy of the church, from the very beginning, because the church condemns homosexuality just as God does in the Holy Scriptures.

He will be killed and resurrected.

In the book of Revelation, we read the description of his death by assassination or possibly from an attack on his estate from another country. It is written that he will suffer a deadly wound and shall miraculously be healed and yet live. This event will apparently cause many to follow and support him. This could be during the events described as the attack on his estate, which comes like a whirlwind from the north. However, considering the nature of his being, an assassination would be a very likely scenario as well.

> And I saw one of his heads as it
> were wounded to death; and his
> deadly wound was healed: and all
> the world wondered after the beast.
> (Revelation 13:3)

We also read of a false prophet that shall arise and shall enforce the worship of the beast. Here again, we see that John mentions the fact that he has a deadly wound and is healed and does live.

> And he exerciseth all the power of the
> first beast before him, and causeth the
> earth and them which dwell therein to
> worship the first beast, whose deadly
> wound was healed.
> (Revelation 13:12)

If all are caused to worship this beast who had the deadly wound, then this must be a man that was wounded to death and not a province of his kingdom. Why would anyone worship a province or worship an image that is set up of a province?

2

Who Will Support Him and Why

As we continue to soar in the realm of technological advancement, we seem to only create more and more toys and gadgets that eat away our time and, ultimately, our life. Have you seen them? You know, the zombies that are constantly entertained by mindless media—such as television, game systems, and, yes, those cell phones that are practically attached to the skin. How easy would it be for such a society to vote for someone if he encouraged such a mindless way of life? If God is not a priority in such a society, we can safely say that God will not be considered in important political decisions when election day comes.

Considering the numerous clues we have studied regarding his identity, we should be able to determine whether or not our modern-day world is ready for him. Would he stand out like an eyesore, or would he blend right in with society and be initially undetectable? Let us look at some factors that would suggest that the world is growing ever closer to the environment that he needs.

The Rise of an Immoral Culture

With a nation of viewers dependant on television sitcoms and Hollywood blockbusters to teach us our culture, what could we expect but the worst case scenario for our future? As millions of people sit in silence watching the screen, writers and producers are given the unique opportunity to mold the mind, as if they were the teachers and instructors of a reeducation camp, slowly changing the values and morals of the masses.

As each decade passes by, it seems that what was previously considered to be the unspeakable is now proclaimed on a loudspeaker. We have now even had a president that supports gay marriage and proudly states that we are not a Christian nation but rather a nation of many gods. And people wonder why the economy along with every other aspect of the nation is falling apart as the president boasts of such things. And the citizens are not even troubled when they see pictures of him kicked back drinking a beer, as all of this is happening.

For such a person to rise and become a world leader and ultimately a god to his subjects, there must first be such a population to subject themselves. If we are to understand that he is a homosexual from scriptural study, then we should naturally expect that homosexuality will be commonplace and well accepted in society when he rises to power. And over the course of only a few decades, we have witnessed multitudes of people who confess homosexuality and the ever increasing promotion of it. Here is a review of the word of God concerning homosexuality.

As mentioned in the Old Testament

Thou shalt not lie with mankind, as with womankind: it is abomination.
(Leviticus 18:22)
If a man also lie with mankind, as he lieth with a woman, both of them have committed an abomination: they shall surely be put to death; their blood shall be upon them. (Leviticus 20:13)
But the men of Sodom were wicked and sinners before the Lord exceedingly.
(Genesis 13:13)

As mentioned in the New Testament

Wherefore God also gave them up to uncleanness through the lusts of their own hearts, to dishonour their own bodies between themselves. (Romans 1:24)

Know ye not that the unrighteous shall not inherit the Kingdom of God? Be not deceived: neither fornicators, nor idolators, nor adulterers, nor effeminate, nor abusers of themselves with mankind. (1 Corinthians 6:9)

So with the knowledge that we have from the word of God concerning homosexuality, how would an elected president claim that he is a Christian and yet support gay marriage? He would either be seriously lacking scriptural knowledge if he were a Christian, by condoning an act of sin, or he quite simply is not a Christian at all. This of course gives a negative depiction of Christianity to the world, especially to those who condemn homosexuality and are unfamiliar with the Holy Scriptures.

Creating the right environment for the rise of the Antichrist has thus far been successful through the means of media and entertainment. We have godless women and men that host popular talk shows on television and sway the opinion of the people. These such hosts promote immorality in the name of freedom and ignorantly depict God as though he accepts homosexuality and all such forms of ungodliness. They also condemn true Christian people and accuse them of being oppressive and self-righteous simply for obeying the word of God.

Television sitcoms and Hollywood films often throw in a gay character, who is funny, successful, and full of life. After adjusting to the character's lifestyle you may realize that you really like them. Soon, you may find yourself defending gay rights in conversation because you remember that fictional character that made you laugh on television. If you have no scriptural knowledge and learn that Christianity does not condone homosexuality, it may seem judgmental and oppressive considering all that you have been lead to believe. If you do have scriptural knowledge and subject yourself to such entertainment, then you have become a victim of the reeducation campaign.

With the continued effort to expand the gay community and to increase the acceptance of the lifestyle through media and entertainment, we are witnessing the realization of an atmosphere that will allow the Antichrist to easily slip in. For example, if a politician were running for office in the 1950s or 1960s, who was a homosexual, how many flags would have gone up? And if there were one running for office today, would it really surprise you if he were elected? How many people suspected that Barack Obama was a Muslim? And yet the majority of the nation put him in the white house.

Along with the support of the homosexual community, we can be certain that anyone supporting abortion, antifamily values, and a dependency on government will line up to elect the beast. Because he will surely promote all of the above. And as the population continues to grow, morals continue to decline. Thus creating a world full of sheep, that will be easily seduced by the flattering words of an ungodly leader.

Considering the fact that the Antichrist is prophesied to make war with the saints, and to overcome them, we can see how such issues would be politically involved. If there are two issues that the church has thus far stood firm on, they are the issues concerning abortion and gay rights. And when the Antichrist rises to power and promotes such ungodliness, he will no doubt come under fire from the church. And being the evil self-righteous dictator that he is, there will surely be consequences of criticism.

As we know from the word of God, we are to hold fast to the commandments of God and to keep the faith. No matter what the cost, even looking death in the face, we must not give up. Jesus Christ was crucified for our sake, and if we be subjected to death for his sake, how could we accept any other option?

A Godless Society

When counting the number of pagan gods in our society, their worshipers may easily turn to a leader with all the answers. When that leader desires to become a god, we must also factor in the growing number of the population that has no god at all. With the fast-paced, media -filled, modern-day world that we live in, many have come to the conclusion that they simply have no time to spare for a god in their life.

With the rising cost of energy and food prices, bundled together with wasted expenses such as satellite TV and costly cell phone bills, many households find themselves working in shifts to pay the bills. Life becomes a morbid cycle of working and watching TV. And time spent at home is mostly in isolation, as the other members of the house are at work when the others are not.

With a lack of God in the lives of many, there will be a multitude of people who will not see what is coming. It still amazes me that there are so many secular people who believe that the world is gradually becoming a better place. And that people such as myself are nothing more than fatalists because we believe the word of God who created the world in which we live.

As we know, when things get really bad, that is when most people seek God. However, it is prophesied in the scriptures that during the tribulation, which will be the most horrific time in history, many shall not seek God, nor shall they repent of their sins. They will in fact blaspheme the name of God because of the plagues that have come upon the earth. There will undoubtedly be many that turn to a leader who opposes God in such situations.

The truth be told, there is no escaping what is inevitable. There are only two options regarding the afterlife. Mortal life in the human body is but a vapor, and there is no promise of tomorrow for any individual. If you consider yourself unaffiliated with God and only regard the cares of this life, what remains of it when you step into eternity? Only regret and shame, and there are no second chances.

If the cares of this life are the priority of the people, then the people will surely turn to anyone who will promise security, prosperity, and a continued way of life that is void of dependency on God. As the desire for material gain increases and the exclusion of God in society continues, it is becoming only the more obvious that such prophetic events could unfold in the near future.

As society increasingly demands that Christians become more tolerant of such things as abortion and homosexuality, it becomes more obvious that the world is less and less tolerant of Christians. What they are really saying to us is, we will not be tolerant of Christians, unless you give up the morals and values that make you a Christian. You cannot condone sin and be a Christian. Therefore the secular world is ultimately saying don't be a Christian.

The gay community expects acceptance from Christianity, though it is a vile and abominable lifestyle according to the word of God. Feminine rights activists argue that abortion is the right of a woman, as if being a woman gives you a right to be a murderer. Ultimately, these two categories of people are only condemning themselves to damnation. However, they do somewhat affect us all by bringing unnecessary judgment upon the land in which they inhabit.

Aside from the secular world increasing in ungodliness, the results of demands for Christians to be tolerant of sin has been somewhat successful. For as much sin as can be found in the world, in some places it can equally be found in the church. We can read the description of such a time in the following verses.

> This know also, that in the last days
> perilous times shall come. For men
> shall be lovers of their own selves,
> covetous, boasters, proud,
> blasphemers, disobedient to parents,
> unthankful, unholy, without natural
> affection, truce breakers, false
> accusers, incontinent, fierce, despisers
> of those that are good, traitors, heady,
> high minded, lovers of pleasures more
> than lovers of God; Having a form of
> godliness, but denying the power
> thereof: from such turn away.
> (2 Timothy 3:1–5)

With the increase of tolerance regarding sinful actions and lifestyles, the church becomes polluted and worldly. In the event of a world crisis, such a church will do according to the world. Answers will be sought from the world leaders because they will not be found of God in such a church. Because God would not be in such a church. Therefore we could witness a major loss of faith in the church when questions and prayers go unanswered.

And what of the millions of members who love to hear prosperity preachers who tell them that they are destined to be blessed in life, rich, and successful? They listen to sermons that are little more than motivational speeches and receive a minimal word of God. Where will their faith level be when the world falls apart? If a super successful minister has been telling them that prosperity is on the way and poverty and famine come, will they even believe in God anymore?

If a multitude of people sit under a preacher who promises earthly prosperity, then it is quite obvious that these people are of the world, seeking the desires of the world such as material gain. When the time comes and things get bad, you can almost envision such a congregation becoming a lynch mob. And the preacher of false promises running for his life as their hard earned money falls out of his pockets.

The fact of the matter is simply this, if there are going to be multitudes of people who are deceived by false christs and multitudes who submit to the Antichrist, it is only because of a lack of studying the word of God. And if there are preachers who hardly teach the word of God during their sermon, they will be held accountable for the lack of knowledge and disinformation that their congregations have received.

So we have numerous categories of people, even including Christians who may easily submit to the Antichrist when he comes. We have clearly read that he will initially honor God, and most likely Allah; however, it is made clear to us that he will actually regard neither God nor Allah. And that he will ultimately make a god of himself. Whatever religion he seems to be affiliated with, he will in fact not be at all. This would mean that he is not a Christian, nor a Muslim, nor a religious Jew. If he happens to initially say that he is one of the above, it will not be true.

There are more than 2 billion Muslims who would never allow a supposed Christian to rule the world. Likewise, there are more than 2 billion Christians who would never allow a supposed Muslim to rule the world. However, there are another 3 billion people that make up the total 7 billion people living on earth that would likely follow someone who is associated with neither religion.

Would a possible scenario be that the Antichrist will campaign to do away with the major religions, and people will love the idea? We know that there have been countless wars, terror attacks, and many lives lost all in the name of religion. Could society be led to believe that the world would be a better place without Christianity and Islam? I'm sure that secular people would love the idea and anyone who could suppress the major religions of the world. I have personally had numerous people tell me that they don't associate themselves with any religion, because more people have died for religion than any other cause.

World Greed and World Power

In our society today, the most important thing in the world seems to be money. Not that it was ever insignificant, but the things that people will do for it have become limitless.

During the 2008 election campaign, there were many young people who admitted that they would literally sell their vote to the highest bidder. Many voted for Barack Obama with the hopes of increased government assistance and free health care.

There have been a number of people in recent years who have allowed business ads and dot-coms to be tattooed on their bodies, even in some cases on their forehead![1] As we know, there have always been prostitutes, strippers, and such establishments that make money off the lusts of the flesh. There has just never been so many and legally operated and advertised. Many of these such businesses are operated on the Internet; they destroy marriages and decimate credit card balances.

Much like the drug dealers who distribute to their own neighborhoods and destroy their own communities for the sake of the dollar, politicians and corporations do the same to the nation. As optimistic as we Christians can be about overturning laws that permit such things as pornography or abortion, it will likely never happen. There is just too much money going into pockets for that to happen.

Money before morals. If it generates large figures, it will endure without fail. Remember the Clinton scandal? The majority of the nation didn't seem to care that he was committing adultery in the oval office. The economy was good at the time, so many people have even suggested that he should be in the White House again, even if he were still committing such acts. So we already know that for the sake of a strong economy and free-flowing money, the citizens will line up to elect anyone, regardless of what they have done and what they are capable of doing.

> But he shall have power over the treasures
> of gold and silver, and over all the precious
> things of Egypt; and the Lybians and the
> Ethiopians shall be at his steps. (Daniel 11:43)

Due to a lack of food and sufficient income, major uprisings began to spread across Middle Eastern countries in January of 2011. Beginning in Tunisia,[2] the protests resulted in the overthrow of government powers in Egypt and Libya. These events raised many eyebrows considering the prophetic verses in the book of Daniel. Could it be that such protests by the citizens of these nations would lead to the rise of the Antichrist in this province? Likely not. As we know, nothing happens in the Middle East unless the United States wants it to.

We involved NATO forces in Libya and UN cease-fire agreements in Syria and were even accused by Iran and Russia of funding and supporting the rebels in the protests. We dictate the actions of Israel, occupy countless regions, and have stretched out a war campaign in Afghanistan and Iraq for more than a decade. If the Antichrist were to rise in the Middle East as a result of the change in governments, it would seem that it would only be the result of a strategic plan, orchestrated by the puppet masters of the western world.

If we study the prophetic visions of Daniel concerning the ram with two horns, which is destroyed by the goat with one horn, we learn that the ram with two horns are the kings of Media and Persia. And the goat with one horn is the king of Grecia. After the king of Grecia falls, four kingdoms rise from the ashes. It is then out of one of these four kingdoms that the Antichrist rises.

Concerning the prophecy of Daniel 11:43, where the Antichrist has power over Egypt and Libya, this is yet a future prophetic event. Because we are told in Daniel 11:40–41 that his kingdom will be attacked by the king of the north, who will come against him like a whirlwind. It is after this attack that he shall enter into these countries.

3

The World Falls Apart to Fall into Place

As foretold in the Holy Scriptures, the world will be thrust into a dark and violent environment, just prior to the time of the end. There will be wars, and rumors of wars. There will be earthquakes, plagues, and famine. And ultimately there will be a time of trouble such as the world has never seen, nor shall ever see again. As we know, there have been continuous wars and conflicts over the years. We have also witnessed in recent years numerous earthquakes that have had devastating consequences.

And yet the time of trouble has not come. We read the description of a possible world war, for nation shall rise against nation and kingdom against kingdom. Will the realization of such perilous times come as a sudden shock, or will we gradually become accustomed to an atmosphere of warfare? Therefore leaving us unaware or uncertain as to whether or not we are witnessing the fulfillment of prophecy? Let us consider the signs that would suggest that there will be many who view the time of the end as business as usual.

The Destabilization of the Mind

Through Hollywood film and gaming entertainment, we can say without any doubt that the youth of the past few generations have been gradually desensitized to violence. With films depicting murder and realistic mutilation and games that place the player in the middle of a war as a combat soldier, killing is becoming just another part of average everyday life.

And there is also desensitization to drug use, alcohol, and every crime under the sun through the cultures of modern music. America has made idols of musicians that promote self-glorification, greed, lust, and even murder. Young impressionable minds across the country view such idols on television and the Internet as they are glamorized and made out to be the picture of modern success.

What could the future hold for such a society that we have so aggressively been pursuing? What could we possibly have to look forward to if the youth today are aspiring to be such idols? The answer is a world full of greedy, selfish idolators who do not regard the values of their ancestors, nor the word of God. And yet the movie theaters are never vacant, and the game systems and CDs fly off the shelf.

While the youth become associated with the visuals of war and horror through the outlets of entertainment, they would actually be rendered useless in the event of unexpected warfare because they have become overweight and unhealthy due to sitting in front of the TV on a regular basis. This is also a major factor in what some are calling the obesity epidemic that America is facing.

Along with such imagery desensitization, we have also become somewhat isolated to each other. With many people communicating by text and status updates on social networking sites, we speak in person much less, yet we know the most minute details of our peers' daily activities. With millions of eyes fixed on small screens, it would seem as though there were an evil conspiracy to cause miotic episodes and a boost in the sales of eyeglasses.

What would millions of media addicts do in the event of an electromagnetic pulse (e.m.p.) going off? It is estimated that in such an event, all forms of communication would be down for at least several weeks. Can you picture it, text addicts without their cell phones, chewing their nails to the quick, even to the bone? Such a media-dependent society would suddenly feel as though they were thrust into the dark ages. And they would most likely act like it as well. It would certainly be a good opportunity to pick up a Bible.

When you think about it, nothing is far-fetched today. And our environment can become chaotic much faster than most people believe. I recall a friend of mine retelling the events of his deployment to New Orleans during the aftermath of Hurricane Katrina. As looters scrambled to steal anything they could get their hands on, bodies lay decomposing in the streets, and there were even people blocking a street and protesting because Popeye's chicken was closed!

Advances in technology have created a very convenient world to live in. But when the day comes that it is suddenly unavailable, our dependency on it will be very inconvenient. And it will be the lack of faith in God that causes the people to panic and to turn to unnecessary acts of violence. But such who have faith and knowledge of what lies ahead shall be prepared for the worst of situations.

In the event of a major disaster or a military strike that would include the loss of computers and communications, the mentality of the masses will be completely alien to the environment. The mentality of such who move into new suburbs, which have been stretched all the way from the city into rural areas, complain about the smell of animals from nearby farms. And yet they expect the milk and the meat to always conveniently be there when they shop. How stable will the population be when such conveniences have suddenly vanished?

Possibly the most interesting question regarding such events is how will a sedated and overmedicated population cope without their happy pills? As we know, there has long been a campaign to create a dependency on drugs. A steady prescription equals steady income for billion-dollar pharmaceutical corporations. A research survey recently reported that an estimated 1 in every 3 American citizens has some form of a mental disorder. What a profitable conclusion for the pharmaceutical corporations!

Imagine a world that is dependent on pills for sleep, anxiety, hyperactive children, pain, stress, and every form of daily discomfort suddenly losing their solution. And all at the same time! If people become animals in the event of a natural disaster, looting stores and risking all for such items as flat screen televisions, what will they do for narcotics that they have become addicted to? It goes without saying that those who have made billions of dollars from medicating the masses will be hiding in secure bunkers as the world falls apart.

The Increase of Sorcery

The subject of sorcery in the modern world is one of much speculation. There are three main theories that describe what exactly the scriptures are referring to when using the word *sorcery*. The word itself translated from the Greek word *pharmakeia* has led many to believe it is speaking of drug use and pharmaceutics. It's definition means (pharmacy) "magic" or "witchcraft." This theory suggests that the sorcery spoken of in the scriptures regarding the latter days are related to the widespread use of narcotics and the never-ending list of symptoms for their use.

There is certainly an evil, dark side of many common drugs that cause psychotic episodes in otherwise normal healthy people, as if the use of a narcotic opens a doorway and pulls the unsuspecting victim into a hellish nightmare. Many users of illegal narcotics have reported similar stories of seeing demons and monsters and having had sudden thoughts of murder and suicide.

Concerning the second theory, it is suggested that the increasing amount of occult activity, interest in psychic readings, and promotion of witches and wizardry in entertainment is the sorcery that is spoken of. There have been numerous movie sagas in recent years that have captured the minds of the youth. Such films have made heroes of witches and wizards and ultimately brought witchcraft into mainstream acceptance.

To the secular world, and even the Christian viewer who is slacking in scriptural study, it would seem to be harmless entertainment. However, it is written in the scriptures that witchcraft, divination, astrology, and all forms of such are an abomination to the Lord. As a Christian, it is impossible to justify viewing such entertainment and taking pleasure in something that is described as an abomination.

Concerning the third theory, it is suggested that the rapid evolution of technology is the result of sorcery. With movable screens at the touch of a finger, worldwide access in the palm of the hand, and mysterious flying crafts in the sky, there is more than enough reason to be suspicious, especially considering that only a century ago we were still riding horses. And communication was only feasible through letters and face-to-face conversation.

Some conspiracies involve the theory that fallen angels, which are considered to be aliens, have given mankind blueprints for the advancement of such technology. In the epistle of Jude, we find mysterious verses that may give credit to such theories. We read of the men of old, referring to the Nephilim that were born of women to the sons of God prior to the flood. We read of how they creep in unaware and also of Enoch, who prophesied of them and their punishment. As for the mysterious flying objects in the sky, we also read of these fallen angels being described as wandering stars, to whom is reserved the blackness of darkness forever.

In the book of Enoch, it is written that the fallen angels corrupted mankind with advanced knowledge prior to the flood. Such things as astrology, charms, and enchantments were given to the daughters of men, whom they took for themselves wives. These women were likely the world's first witches, and these such events were likely the birth of witchcraft. All three of these theories regarding sorcery are certainly increasing with time.

Scenarios of Natural Disasters

In recent years, we have been witness to the catastrophic results of severe weather patterns and how they quickly plunge our world into a chaotic state. Hurricanes and tornadoes wreak havoc, leaving towns and communities in shambles. Many seek to satisfy questions as to whether or not God is suddenly angry with our nation. The truth be told, we have long had policies and practices in our nation that would anger God.

Due to troubling dreams that my wife had in early 2012 concerning a massive earthquake, we were prompted to search out others who may have had similar prophetic dreams. The results were shocking, finding that many people across the nation had recently experienced similar dreams, some of them even having identical details. The study of these prophetic dreams reveals a grim suggestion that there will be a monstrous mega quake on the New Madrid fault.

Over two hundred years ago, the nation experienced a series of monster earthquakes and aftershocks that stretched out over the course of several months. The damages from the New Madrid earthquakes were minimal, considering the lack of population and development. However, the powerful quakes caused the Mississippi river to flow backward, church bells in Boston to ring, and the sidewalks of Washington, DC, to crack open.[1]

Today, it is estimated that such an earthquake would leave more than seven million people homeless and thousands dead. It would likely cause a division in the nation, taking out crucial bridges and routes for delivery that are traveled every day. Such a disaster could change the entire nation and turn the world we know upside down. The lack of food delivery could cause panic abroad, and the devastated cities could experience looting, rioting, and martial law. Ultimately, a nearly bankrupted government could not sufficiently meet the needs for humanitarian aid, cleanup, and rebuilding.

Possibly the worst aspect to such a scenario would be outside of our nation. If such a natural disaster occurred and the nation were suddenly crippled, we would become extremely vulnerable to anyone who would wish to attack us. Whether it be a military strike, full enemy invasion, or a sudden terror attack, it would be very challenging circumstances in the midst of disaster. Depending on the magnitude of the attack, it could even be the straw that broke the camel's back.

The same case could be made for the eruption of Mount Saint Helens. The results would be equally devastating, with ash clouds blocking out the sun for a long period. We would experience the loss of crops and air quality and again the worst case scenario involving the enemy threat. Eventually such disasters will happen. It is foretold that the whole earth will be shaken, both the heaven and the earth. It is easy to think that we will never experience such perilous times, with the mentality that has evolved in our nation. No matter how safe and secure we feel, we are only fooling ourselves if we write off the possibilities. Desperate times call for desperate measures. In the event of a major crisis, the loss of liberty can occur in the blink of an eye. The laws are written, everything is in place, and at any given moment, we are only a crisis away from becoming citizens without rights.

The president becomes a dictator, and military has the right to take over all highways, farmland, schools, and any such property seen fit, including vehicles, farm equipment, firearms, phones, and any other communication devices and on and on. How easy would it be for society to submit to a leader with such unchecked power? If the government is overseeing the distribution of food and shelter, many will happily do as they are told just for the sake of feeding themselves and their family.

With knowledge becoming more widespread regarding the unconstitutional laws that are now in place, there is a growing number of citizens who have gone into survival mode. As many as can afford to go off the grid have done so, making preparations to supply their own power source for electricity and communication. Reality TV has even given viewers valuable tips for survival by giving a glimpse inside the lives of families that farm their land and produce their own food and spend their recreational time becoming sharp shooters with AR-15s and sniper rifles.

In the event of disaster and total government control, there is no question as to who is safe and who is doomed. Those who are off the grid and self-sufficient will keep on keeping on. But those who are in heavily populated cities and completely dependent on the government will take whatever is dished out to them. And tyranny and destruction will likely come as a sudden shock to them.

A Massive Loss of Life

Earthquakes and tsunamis in the last decade have claimed the lives of hundreds of thousands of people worldwide. While the number of deaths has been shocking, and terrible, it is nothing in comparison to what lies ahead. As the prophetic time clock ticks on, we will surely witness more and more disasters that increase in both severity and the number of human casualties.

The scriptures foretell not only of earthquakes but of wars that will eliminate billions of people from among the living. One significant war that is likely to soon happen is the war of Gog, the land of Magog.

> Persia, Ethiopia, and Libya with them;
> all of them with shield and helmet:
> Go'mer, and all his bands; the house of
> To -gar'mah of the north quarters, and
> all his bands: and many people with thee.
> (Ezekiel 38:5–6)

With all that is going on in the Middle East, it would seem that almost anything could happen at any time. With Israel under constant threat from terror organizations and the countdown to Iran having nuclear weapons, such a war would come as no surprise if it were in the headlines tomorrow. This event spoken of in Ezekiel, foretells of a supernatural intervention by God, and describes the result as a massive death toll.

> And I will plead against him with pestilence and with blood; and I will rain upon him, and upon his bands, and upon the many people that are with him, an overflowing rain, and great hailstones, fire, and brimstone. (Ezekiel 38:22)

This event will produce an unprecedented amount of dead bodies. In the following verses, we read the description of a massive air assault and a rather lengthy period in which the bodies will be recovered and buried.

> Thou shalt ascend and come like a storm, thou shalt be like a cloud to cover the land, thou, and all thy bands, and many people with thee. (Ezekiel 38:9)
> And seven months shall the house of Israel be burying of them, that they may cleanse the land. (Ezekiel 39:12)

The widespread warfare is foretold in the breaking of the seals and the release of the four horsemen of the apocalypse.

> And there went out another horse that was red: and power was given to him that sat thereon to take peace from the earth, and that they should kill one another: and there was given unto him a great sword. (Revelation 6:4)

This verse seems to give us a vision of more than war, or even world war. If peace has been taken from the earth, we can envision worldwide anarchy and murder. Not only will wars be raging, but there will likely be violence in the streets of every major city across the world. In the next verse, we read of the opening of the fourth seal and the vision of the fourth horseman of the apocalypse.

> And I looked, and behold a pale horse: and his name that sat on him was Death, and Hell followed with him. And power was given unto them over the fourth part of the earth, to kill with sword, and with hunger, and with death, and with the beasts of the earth. (Revelation 6:8)

The common interpretation of the verse regarding the fourth horseman is that one quarter of the earths population will be killed, because it says that power was given to them over the fourth part of the earth. However, considering that it says that power was given to them over *the* fourth part of the earth rather than *a* fourth part of the earth, could this be a certain province or section of the earth? In chapter 7, John writes that he has seen four angels standing on the four corners of the earth, holding the four winds of the earth, so there are obviously four parts that make up the earth, but which one would be considered the fourth part?

Another oddity that raises questions when reading this verse is the fact that both *Death* and *Hell* are capitalized as though they were names of literal beings. Is there actually an angel of death, such as the grim reaper? What did John see to make him say that Hell followed with him? Did he see a wall of fire behind the rider of the horse, or did he see the host of hell coming forth to terrorize humanity?

In the book of Zechariah, we read of his vision regarding what would seem to be the four horsemen of the apocalypse. He sees the same number of horses and also the same colored horses that were in John's vision. However, unlike John's vision, in this account we are given insight as to who they are and where they go. The angel of the Lord tells Zechariah that they are the four spirits of the heavens, which go forth from standing before the Lord of all the earth (Ze. 6:5).

In the book of Revelation, the rider of the pale horse, which is the fourth horseman, is identified as Death. Thus,

Death is an actual being and one of the four spirits of the heavens, which stand before the Lord of all the earth. This interpretation is fitting because we know that Jesus was given power over death and hell. But who are the other three spirits of the heavens whom stand before the Lord?

The common interpretation regarding the identity of the rider of the white horse is that he is the Antichrist. In the book of Revelation, he is described as having a bow and having been given a crown and that he went forth conquering. However, considering the insight from the book of Zechariah, this interpretation becomes puzzling. If the four horsemen are identified as being the four spirits of the heavens which stand before the Lord, this would mean that the Antichrist is one of the four spirits and that he is standing before the Lord.

Below is a chart to better visualize the comparison of the four horsemen as they are described in the books of Zechariah and Revelation. We see in the book of Zechariah a description of where they go and in the book of Revelation what they have come forth to do in the earth.

The Four Spirits **Zechariah**		The Four Horsemen **Revelation**
Direction not given. Possibly because it covers the entire earth.	**Red Horse**	Takes peace from the earth, that they should kill one another.
Goes forth into the North country.	**Black Horse**	Pair of balances in his hand. A measure of wheat for a penny, and three measures of barley for a penny.
Follows after the black horse, goes into the North country.	**White Horse**	Rider has a bow and is given a crown, and goes forth conquering and to conquer.
Goes forth toward the South country, and to walk to and fro through the earth.	**Grisled/Pale Horse**	Rider is identified as Death, and Hell follows with him. Given power over the fourth part of the earth.

Whatever interpretation you consider, the events which John described are going to be unimaginable. And there will be no escaping it, nor altering it, for whatsoever God has spoken, so shall it come to pass.

4

The Mark of the Beast

As well known as the four horsemen of the apocalypse is the prophecy concerning the mark of the beast. As technology advances, the possible methods of implementation increase. When social security was established, countless believers were undoubtedly suspicious, as they learned that all citizens would have a unique number assigned to their name. The buzz of such a mandatory law has once again surfaced and raised legitimate concerns.

Those who have read through the thousands of pages of the national health care act, also known as Obama care, have stated that upon its implementation, all citizens that wish to receive health care will be required to have a small microchip implanted under their skin. For the purposes of identification and medical history, this implant is projected to be mandatory for all health care recipients by the year 2017.[1]

As diabolical as it sounds, like a plot to take over the world from a low budget science fiction film, such a law will inevitably be established. And the sad part about it is that the masses will not see it for what it truly is. And those who know the truth will quickly be written off as conspiracy theorists and raving fanatics by a blind society that has become an enslaved people.

The Mystery of the Mark

If someone were to ask you, "What is the mark of the beast?" you would quickly tell them that it is the number 666, would you not? This would likely be the answer that 9 out of 10 believers would give. However, it is not the correct answer because we do not yet know what this mark is. In the book of Revelation, we read that there are three different options that will be available. Let us look at the verse that describes these options.

> And that no man might buy or sell,
> save he that had the mark, *or* the
> name of the beast, *or* the number of
> his name. (Revelation 13:17, italics mine)

This is not the only verse that tells us that there are three separate ways of condemning ourselves to the submission of the beast. We are given the same description in the following verse, when John describes his vision of those who overcome, by not submitting to the beast.

> And I saw as it were a sea of glass
> mingled with fire: and them that had
> gotten the victory over the beast, *and*
> over his image, *and* over his mark,
> *and* over the number of his name,
> stand on the sea of glass, having the
> harps of God. (Revelation 15:2, italics mine)

So if this mark is a separate option from his name or the number of his name, it cannot be his name or the number of his name. So what is it? Could it be some form of an icon that would be globally recognized like a trademark? Would it be in the form of a tattoo or a brand or some other type of permanent marking?

In the past few decades, we have witnessed a major increase in the amount of people who have tattoos. Where it was once an oddity to see ink-covered skin in public places such as the supermarket, the tables have now turned, and there seems to be a piece of artwork on nearly everyone you see. I myself am among them, having been a victim of blending in with society before I was saved.

In a society that has anything and everything tattooed permanently in their skin, how easily would the masses accept the mark of a leader in the form of a tattoo? Many would likely welcome it and consider it to be just another addition to a growing collection of tattoos. While ink-covered skin used to be only common among bikers, gang members, and rock stars, it has become a part of nearly every modern culture. Even good Christian people today are getting tattoos, including ministers that preach from the pulpit. These are worldly Christians, going along with the rest of the world. Once the church begins to look like the world, there is something wrong with that church, is there not?

There are only a few historical examples in the Bible that have involved a mysterious mark being put upon man. Ironically, the purpose of the mark was to ensure that whosoever was wearing it would not be killed. In the book of Revelation, we read the description of the locusts which come out of the pit. And how they torment men for five months, and yet the men do not die.

> And in those days shall men seek death, and shall not find it; and shall desire to die, and death shall flee from them. (Revelation 9:6)

Wait a minute, we just read in chapter 6 that the identity of the fourth horseman was Death and that he was physically on the earth. So how could it be that men would seek death and not find it? Considering that the verse says that *physical* death will flee from them, it seems that Death is instructed not to take those who have this mark, the mark of the beast. The first instance of a man receiving a mark is found in Genesis, and the mark was to prevent an untimely death.

> And the Lord said unto him, therefore
> whosoever slayeth Cain, vengeance
> shall be taken on him sevenfold. And
> the Lord set a mark upon Cain, lest any
> finding him should kill him. (Genesis 4:15)

Considering the many strange circumstances that surround Cain, I am really surprised that he has never been named among the suspects of those who might be the Antichrist. There is no written record of his death, as there were of the others in his time. He was the world's first murderer, and the devil is described as being a murderer from the beginning (Jo. 8:44). Cain killed his brother, and during the time of the Antichrist, every man's sword will be against his brother. And it is expected that Enoch and Elijah will return as the two witnesses that prophesy in the last days, so it would not be that much of a stretch to consider Cain a suspect.

Another instance of a mark being issued to prevent one from death is found in the book of Ezekiel. Before God executes his judgment, he requires that the righteous receive a mark to keep them from being killed.

> And the Lord said unto him, go through
> the midst of the city, through the midst of
> Jerusalem, and set a mark upon the
> foreheads of the men that sigh and that
> cry for all the abominations that be done
> in the midst thereof. (Ezekiel 9:40)

> Slay utterly old and young, both maids,
> and little children, and women: but come
> not near any man upon whom is the mark;
> and begin at my sanctuary. Then they
> began at the ancient men which were
> before the house. (Ezekiel 9:6)

While many theories surround the mark of the beast, no one can say for certain what it will look like. The possibility of an implantable microchip, which is the size of a grain of rice, is worth considering. However, since it is referred to as a mark, it will surely be something that is visible, whereas a small chip under the skin would not. We do know that it is something that is in the skin, like that of a tattoo. The following verse makes this clear.

> And he causeth all, both small and
> great, rich and poor, free and bond,
> to receive a mark *in* their right hand,
> or *in* their foreheads. (Revelation 13:16, italics mine)

The Shepherd of Lost Souls

Having considered a few possibilities regarding the mark of the beast, we will now consider the name of the beast. While it remains unknown to us, there are many words and titles given in scripture when referring to him. We know that his number is 666 and that it is the number of his name. Could it be that there are six letters in his first, middle, and last name? Or is there a new number system like that of social security that will emerge? Such as that of a microchip implant upon birth? If it were a number system such as this, he would likely be among the first seven hundred to receive his number out of the billions of people that make up the earth.

Upon my study of the numerous commonly known names that are used to describe him, I have stumbled upon one that I believe has been overlooked. In the second epistle to the Thessalonians, Paul is writing about the Antichrist when he does something quite strange. In the middle of a verse, he has capitalized the word *Wicked*, as though it were a name rather than a word of reference.

After discovering this, I first took a look at several other Bibles to ensure that it wasn't a misprint. I found that this word has been capitalized in the middle of Paul's sentence, in every King James Bible that I checked. Additionally, I searched Strong's exhaustive concordance of the Bible and found that of the approximately 330 verses that include the word *wicked*, this is the only one that has capitalized the word. And it was capitalized in the concordance as well.

The Greek word for *wicked* is *anomos*. Its definition is "lawless," not subject to Jewish law, and by implication, it describes a gentile. This could support the theory that the Antichrist is not a Jew, but a gentile. Another interesting point is that the word *wicked* is made up of six letters. While it is very unlikely that anyone would be named Wicked, it is interesting that it is capitalized mid verse, and that it contains six letters. Let us take a look at the verse, along with a list of all his names and titles.

> And then shall that Wicked be revealed, whom the Lord shall consume with the spirit of his mouth, and shall destroy with the brightness of his coming.
> (2 Thessalonians 2:8)

* *The little horn* (Daniel 7:8). He is a small king. He rises with a small people or nation.
* *A king of fierce countenance* (Daniel 8:23). He is a king with a dreadful, powerful appearance.
* *The man of sin* (2 Thess. 2:3). He is a fierce king, who is utterly consumed with sin.
* *The son of perdition* (2 Thess. 2:3). He is a fierce king who is consumed with sin and was born and destined for damnation.
* *That Wicked* (2 Thess. 2:8). He is a fierce king who is consumed with sin and destined for damnation. Who is a lawless gentile?
* *The Antichrist* (1 John 2:22). He is a fierce king who is consumed with sin and destined for damnation. And he will be the opponent of the Messiah.

* *The beast* (Rev. 13:3). He is a fierce king who is consumed with sin and destined for damnation. And he will be the opponent of the Messiah and a blood-thirsty beast.

A few examples regarding the titles (son of perdition and that Wicked) clearly tell us that he is born for the sole purpose of fulfilling end-time prophecy. Also, he is predestined to the condemnation of eternal damnation. Below are the verses for these references.

> The wicked are estranged from the womb:
> they go astray as soon as they be born,
> speaking lies. (Psalm 58:3)
> The righteous shall rejoice when he seeth
> the vengeance: he shall wash his feet in
> the blood of the wicked. (Psalm 58:10)

With all the many names given him, Wicked is the only one that is capitalized. Whether he be called the beast, the Antichrist, or any other name, this is the only one capitalized. Time will tell all, and perhaps the many mysterious names and titles will make sense. According to Paul, we will be able to identify him in his time, and he shall be revealed (2 Thess. 2:5) However, those who are unrighteous shall not know even still, for we are told that God will send a strong delusion, that they might believe a lie (2 Thess. 2:11)

To Depend on God or Government

If we are to view the book of Revelation as a series of events that are in exact order, it would seem confusing to say the least. For example, in chapter 7, John sees the saints which came out of great tribulation, and the great tribulation has not begun at this point. Also, it is only after all the seal judgments, trumpet judgments, and vial judgments that we see the destruction of Mystery Babylon. And yet there are multitudes of people standing afar off mourning for her.

It is impossible to consider just how many people have been slain from the plagues, which resulted from the judgments. However, during the last seven years before Christ returns, there will yet remain multitudes of people who will accept the mark of the beast. Because we are told that the whole world wondered after the beast and worshiped the dragon, which gave him his power (Rev. 13:3–4).

So we know that there will be a multitude of blind sheep that literally find themselves in awe of the Antichrist. Such people are going to willingly accept the mark of the beast. These people will be ungodly, worldly, followers of the evil imaginations of the heart, and sinners of every variety who seek any alternative path to avoid the laws of God. This will be the first category of people who accept the mark.

The second category will be those who have heard the truth and not received the love of it. Therefore God will send a strong delusion that they might believe a lie (2 Thess. 2:11) . There will also likely be Christians who accept the mark of the beast because Paul warns in his epistle to the Thessalonians to "Let no man deceive you by any means," and he goes on to say that there will be a falling away first before that man of sin is revealed.

This second group of people are similar to the first, the only difference being that they label themselves as Christians. These are the Christians who resemble the world and follow the sinful trends of the world—those who play for both teams so to speak, those who have been deceived and led astray by strange doctrines and have corrupted the truth of the word of God. Such people that live according to the world have deceived themselves and such as that subscribe to false doctrines have been deceived by others. Seeing as that they already believe a lie, they will continue doing so.

The third category will be those who are unaffiliated with any religion, and will remain unaffiliated to the end. These are the people who have no time in their life for a god and who love and worship themselves rather than God. Such people will submit to an evil government and accept the mark of the beast as though things were business as usual. They believe in nothing and will fall for anything, just to keep the world turning.

The fourth category may include all of the above—anyone that will submit for the sake of their life. If a law is established that they are to receive the mark of the beast and not doing so is punishable by death (Rev. 13:15), they will do so to avoid execution. And all such people that depend on the government for order, for food, for health care, and for other benefits will likely submit.

However convenient it may seem at the time, to accept a mark as an alternative to execution, the truth be told, it will be the worst deal in the history of humanity. While choosing life would seem to be a no-brainer, life will only go on for a few more years. So to put it in clear perspective, the choice will be simply this, a few more years of life on earth, which is being plagued with the worst events in history, and then eternal damnation or a sudden death that allows you to escape the horrors of the plagues and the entry into eternal life in the presence of God.

It will be the ultimate showdown of the battle between the spirit and the flesh. Our human body will struggle to live on, and yet our spirit will be damned for eternity if we choose to accept the mark of the beast. And of the many reasons why people will be willing to submit, none of them are going to be excused by God. If one must starve to death due to the ineligibility of receiving food, then so be it. Likewise, if anyone must die in any manner to avoid the mark of the beast, so be it.

Jesus Christ was crucified an innocent and sinless man. He could have at any time avoided this, but for the sake of all mankind, he submitted to death. Directly after the warning not to take the mark of the beast, John hears a voice from heaven, which tells him to write: "Blessed are the dead which die in the Lord from henceforth" (Rev.14:13). This is likely because they have become martyrs and have laid down their life for Jesus Christ, just as he laid down his life for all of us.

In the next chapter, we will consider what the world will look like under the system of the mark of the beast, what technology it will require, and what tools are already available for its implementation. Also, we will consider the progression toward a global one-world order and how the inhabitants of the world will easily adjust to it as time continues to reveal the fact that it is coming, and coming fast at that.

5

Technology to Control the Masses

There have been countless prophetic visions and near-death experiences in the past few decades that have revealed a world of technology that has since come to pass. In numerous documented events, there have been subjects who shared similar experiences, such as having been shown futuristic events by angelic beings through what they described as a small picture box. We would recognize this today as something similar to a portable DVD player.

One example is that of a man who died in a sudden tragic accident in the mid 1970s. After having been revived, he had many things to tell regarding his afterlife encounter with the angelic beings. He spoke of a biological engineer who would create a unique virus that would be used in the production of microchips. These microchips would eventually be mandatory for mankind to have implanted under the skin. He then described this individual as having become very rich and powerful as a result of these microchips. He goes on to describe him as a likely candidate for the office of the Antichrist.

Microchips and Satellites

The invention of the microchip is credited to Jack Kilby,[1] who was born in 1923 in Jefferson City, Missouri. He created the first integrated circuit while working for Texas Instruments in 1958. Since that time, microchips have become an essential part of our daily life. When the word *microchip* comes up, most of us think of computers, cell phones, game systems, etc. However, it goes much deeper than that.

Microchips have now found a home in everything from football helmets to toilets. And depending on where you shop for clothing, you could even be wearing a microchip yourself, with certain retailers including a microchip the size of a grain of sand in the tags of clothing items. With computerized restrooms, Aqua One Technologies has presented a toilet that has an automatic shutoff in the event of a leak. And Japanese company Toto has a smart toilet that reads health-related data from the user's urine and sends the information to the user's physician.[2] Another odd use of modern microchips has been presented by a company in Pennsylvania and is called the memory medallion. It is a coin-sized steel-encased microchip for tombstones.[3] It tells the story of the deceased in photos, audio, and video. It can be activated when a visitor points their Internet-enabled cell phone at it.

The microchips that are raising eyebrows and creating conspiracy theories however are the likes of those created by such companies as Applied Digital Solutions and Alien Technologies. Applied Digital Solutions is the company that created the highly controversial verichip, also known as the Digital Angel. With the use of GPS/satellite communications, the Verichip[4] can be implanted in both animals and humans for tracking and location purposes.

While millions of pets have been implanted with the RFID (radio frequency identification) chips, there are now a growing number of people who are receiving these implants as well. With the FDA-approved microchips, there are many possibilities being promoted, such as mandating the implants for all US soldiers and eventually all US citizens through the new health care system. It is proposed that all health care recipients will be required to pay a monthly fee for the use of their implants. All the patient's health records will be contained within the chip and can be reviewed by medical staff by simply using a RFID scanner.

Eventually, it is highly likely that all human beings will be required to fuse this technology into their person. With all the advantages that are being presented, such as medical and financial uses, we could easily see the evolution of a chipped society quickly come to pass. If a new monetary system is established and a one- world currency presented, it will likely involve the use of a card or microchip and be completely digital.

When the new monetary system is established, multitudes of people will be forced to accept an implant in order to maintain a banking account. As we know, no one will be able to buy or sell lest they have the mark of the beast. We are witnessing the worldwide collapse of the current monetary system. By the time the world powers have completed the economic crisis that they have created, society will be willing to accept any solution that they have to offer.

What many people do not realize is that they can already be tracked and easily located with the use of microchips and the thousands of satellites that are in orbit. Really, the only difference between having a microchip implant is that you will be aware that you are being monitored and tracked. Right now you can be tracked by your cell phone, and your conversations can be recorded even when your not on the phone.

Your vehicle can be tracked and located with GPS, clothing with RFID chips, etc. It is unbelievable to watch society willingly step into such an obvious snare, and what is the advantage? You have a portable phone. You don't get lost or ask for directions with your vehicle's GPS. How did our ancestors survive? What would they think of our modern technology? They would probably view us as helpless simpletons who have to depend on technology to even use a toilet.

Scalar Weapons and Weather Modification

With the increase of bizarre weather and extreme storm systems, there has been a lot of buzz about the possibilities of weather modification. Super powers such as Russia and the United States have become suspect of possessing and using advanced scalar wave technology to induce intense weather patterns. Awareness of the US government program titled HAARP, which is based in Alaska, has become widespread. And yet little more has been learned regarding its nature.

The knowledge of scalar wave technology is traced back to the time of Nicola Tesla[5] who discovered how to harness scalar waves from one transmitter to another without the use of wiring. He was financially supported for the works that he conducted in his laboratories on Long Island and in Colorado Springs by JP Morgan. But Morgan cut off financing, considering he would have lost all his income from electricity if Tesla were capable of producing free energy for the masses.

At the time of his death, Tesla's documents were reportedly recovered by the FBI and considered to be top secret. However, the Russians and the Germans had supposedly already obtained knowledge of his advanced technologies, such as antigravity technology, which is suspected to be the origin of modern UFOs, a death ray weapon, and an earthquake-inducing machine.

The many suspected capabilities of scalar wave technology are mind-boggling and sound like the work of a science fiction novel. The capabilities include the creation of a nuclear-type explosion at any location on earth with the use of laser and particle beams, with the induction of powerful earthquakes, severe thunderstorms, and even mind control via subliminal messages from satellites.

Biblically speaking, many people believe that subliminal messages and broadcasts via satellites may play a major role in what is considered to be the coming great deception. "The Voice of God Weapon," which evolved from the top secret government project known as MK ULTRA,[6] has led conspiracy theorists to suspect that such capabilities will be used to one day convince the masses that aliens are communicating with earth, and this would prove to the world that there is intelligent life in space. And ultimately, this would tie in to the theory that the government will explain the vanishing of millions of Christians around the world in the rapture.

Concerning earthquakes and weather modification, much has happened in the past few years to give credibility to the existence and use of scalar wave technology. Just after New Year's Day in 2011, an estimated five thousand red wing blackbirds died in midair and dropped from the skies over Beebee Arkansas.[7] If that was not bizarre enough, there was also an estimated one hundred thousand dead drum fish that washed ashore on nearby riverbanks. Researchers that have studied the use and effects of scalar wave technology suggest that scalar waves could destroy animals that have small brains if they were in the line of fire of the scalar waves.

Conspiracy theorists find it very interesting that this odd event occurred in such close proximity to the New Madrid fault. It is also interesting that it occurred in the year that would mark the two hundredth anniversary of the great earthquakes that rocked this area in 1811 and 1812. Also, this area of the Midwest experienced the worst outbreak of tornadoes in recorded history, beginning only two months after the bizarre death of the five thousand blackbirds and the one hundred thousand drum fish.

With the question of weather warfare, there is also the buzz about chem trails. Have you noticed those white lines that checkerboard our skies today and seem to linger for hours? At first glance, and without putting any thought into it, most would assume that they are the contrails from jetliners. The difference is that contrails are condensation from the exhaust of aircraft engines, which create long thin artificial clouds.

Chem trails however are trails left by aircraft that contain chemical or biological agents. While the theory continues to grow in the United States, the government insists that the trails are nothing more than condensation, and the United States air force states that chem trails are nothing more than a hoax, or a conspiracy theory. But as we know, only mindless sheep believe everything that the government tells them to believe.

Russia on the other hand has had the decency to acknowledge the fact that chem trails are real, and they have made this information public to their citizens.[8] On October 18, 2009, it was reported that the mayor of Moscow announced that there would be no snow, thanks to the use of chem trails. With a price tag of a few million dollars, the Moscow city council agreed to pay the Russian air force to spray a combination of cement powder and silver iodide above the clouds outside of Moscow.

The result of doing this would cause the clouds to dump their payload of snow outside of Moscow. Therefore the streets of Moscow would only have a dusting of snow, which saves both road crews and commuters from the nightmares of winter travel. It has also been reported that on certain holidays, such as Victory day in May and City day in September, Russia keeps the skies blue and clear with the use of chem trails. If there is a forecast for rain, or snow, Russia is more than capable of stopping it.

If Russia not only acknowledges the existence of chem trails but also the fact that they use them, does this not clearly tell us that chem trails are a reality and not just some strange conspiracy theory? And it goes without saying that if Russia is experimenting with and using chem trails, so is the United States. The fact that the United States denies any knowledge of chem trails should make us ask ourselves, what are they using them for that they have to lie about it? Since they openly lie, we have to consider the most grim possibilities.

If society must be broken down and the world in desperate situations to accept a new world order, there will have to be serious changes made that affect our daily lives. In 2012, the Midwest experienced the worst drought in more than fifty years. There was a serious loss of annual crops due to the lack of rain and the extremely hot temperatures. It is estimated that some 1,700 counties in more than 36 states were legally declared natural disaster areas due to the drought.

This loss of crops will substantially raise food prices in the future, and if the drought continues, they could skyrocket. Could this be the work of a generated crisis or is it just a natural occurrence? Should we suspect such conspiracies to play out at the hands of world powers? Of course we should! If we are leading up to the most brutal, controlling world government that has ever existed, we need to open our eyes and review the evidence that is right in front of our noses.

While the chem trails that linger in the skies for hours speak for themselves, they are not the only visible evidence that can be seen when you look up. In 2009, many people began seeing bizarre cloud formations. Some people described them as being "apocalyptic looking" and very foreboding. After being reviewed and verified as a new cloud type, they were named Asperatus clouds in 2009.[9]

Having personally seen these clouds for myself in Missouri, I can certainly attest to the fact that they are quite bizarre in appearance. They look like raging waves in the sea, and in pictures that I have taken of them, they look fake, like the works of special effects in the movies. And they look totally out of place in the sky. Possibly stranger than their appearance is their nature. While they manage to cover the entire sky when they come into view and give a strong impression that a bad storm is coming, nothing ever happens—not a drop of rain, not a strong wind, absolutely nothing happens.

A Call for Global Government

The establishment of the United Nations was a significant step toward global government. Having come into existence on October 24, 1945, the United Nations headquarters is located in New York City and was initiated by American president Franklin D. Roosevelt. The creation of the UN was an attempt to succeed in the prevention of war and disarmament, where the league of nations, which was initiated by American president Woodrow Wilson, had failed.

Today, there are 193 member states that have been swallowed up by the organization. Here at home, the UN has control of all American landmarks, such as the Statue of Liberty, Independence hall, Monticello, Yellowstone, the Grand Canyon, the Great Smoky Mountains, and on and on. What is more disturbing than the amount of American land that is under UN control is what they could soon potentially do with our money. In the second term for President Obama, which began in 2012, it is expected that the UN will tap into the pockets of Americans for tobacco taxes, carbon taxes, and numerous other taxes that will be redistributed around the globe.

Along with the ridiculous taxes, we also have the United Nations Arms Trade Treaty to contend with. Negotiated at a global conference in New York City in July of 2012, it will allow the UN to regulate the international trade of conventional weapons. Of the 193 member states, there were only 24 countries that abstained from the treaty. Surprisingly the US was one of them. It is assumed that Obama backed down due to intense pressure from such organizations as the National Rifle Association. However, now that Obama is in his second presidential term, he will have much more freedom to do as he pleases.

With the prophetic time clock ticking at a quickening pace, it only becomes more evident that we are growing dangerously closer to serious changes. And when world leaders are openly discussing a new world order, we should certainly take them serious. Below is a list of quotes from around the world that reveal to us that something is definitely in the works behind the scenes.

> His task will be to develop an overall strategy for America in this period when, really, a new world order can be created. It's a great opportunity, it isn't just a crisis.
> (Henry Kissinger speaking of Obama,[10] CNBC interview)

Today America would be outraged if UN troops entered Los Angeles to restore order. Tomorrow they will be grateful. When presented with this scenario, individual rights will be willingly relinquished for the guarantee of their well being granted to them by the world government.

(Henry Kissinger speaking of America,[11] address to Bilderberg meeting)

All nations must come together to build a stronger global regime.

(Barack Obama on new world order,[12] presidential speech)

Climate bill will help bring about global governance…but it is the awareness itself that will drive the change and one of the ways it will drive the change is through global governance and global agreements.

(Al Gore on new world order,[13] speech on climate change)

We need a global new deal…a grand bargain between the countries and continents of this world.

(UK Prime Minister Gordon Brown,[14] speech before G20 summit)

We have before us the opportunity to forge for ourselves and for future generations a new world order… When we are successful,

> and we will be, we have a real chance at this
> new world order. An order in which a
> credible United Nations can use its peace
> keeping role to fulfill the promise and vision
> of the UN's founders.
> (George Bush Sr. on new world order, [15] televised speech)
>
> We must move as quickly as possible to a
> one world government, one world religion,
> under a one world leader.
> (Robert Mueller, former assistant secretary general of UN[16])

Not only do we have evidence that there are secret plans being laid out regarding the future one world order, but we see that they have been in the works for quite some time. Let us consider what former presidents and US leaders have said concerning a secret agenda, dating as far back as more than a century ago.

> Some of the biggest men in the United States,
> in the field of commerce and manufacture, are
> afraid of something. They know that there is a
> power somewhere so organized, so subtle, so
> watchful, so interlocked, so complete, so
> pervasive, that they had better not speak
> above their breath when they speak in
> condemnation of it. (Woodrow Wilson[17])

> For we are opposed, around the world, by a monolithic and ruthless conspiracy, that relies primarily on covert means for expanding it's sphere of influence, on infiltration instead of invasion, on subversion instead of elections, on intimidation instead of free choice, on guerrillas by night, instead of armies by day, it is a system which has conscripted, vast material and human resources into the building of a tightly knit, highly efficient machine that combines military, diplomatic, intelligence, economic, scientific, and political operations. It's preparations are concealed, not published. It's mistakes are buried, not headlined. It's dissenters silenced, not praised. (JFK speech[18])
>
> All of us will ultimately be judged on the effort we have contributed to building a New World Order. (Robert Kennedy [19])

If these quotes from world leaders are not enough to sell you on the fact that there is a new world order in the works, maybe you need it written in stone. In that case, for the sake of proving this, it is in fact literally written in stone, right here at home in the United States of America.

Known as the American Stonehenge, or more commonly referred to as the Georgia Guidestones,[20] in Elbert County, Georgia, stands the mysterious granite monument with apocalyptic references. Erected in 1979, an unknown person under the pseudonym RC Christian hired Elberton Granite Finishing Company to build the large structure. Standing nearly twenty feet tall, a total of six granite slabs weighing 237,746 pounds, stand astronomically aligned.

The astronomical features include a channel through the stone indicating the celestial pole. A horizontal slot indicates travel of the sun. And sunbeam through the capstone marks noontime throughout the year. On the edges of the square have names of four ancient languages written on them— Babylonian, Classical Greek, Sanskrit, and Ancient Egyptian. And in modern language, there are eight listed, including English, Spanish, Swahili, Hindi, Hebrew, Arabic, Chinese, and Russian. A separate tablet in the ground reads the following: "Let these be guide stones to an age of reason." And on the guide stones themselves, the following ten guidelines for humanity are written.

1. Maintain humanity under 500,000,000 in perpetual balance with nature.
2. Guide reproduction wisely- improving fitness and diversity.
3. Unite humanity with a living new language.
4. Rule passion-faith-tradition- and all things with tempered reason.
5. Protect people and nations with fair laws and just courts.

6. Let all nations rule internally resolving external disputes in a world court.

7. Avoid petty laws and useless officials.

8. Balance personal rights with social duties.

9. Prize truth-beauty-love- seeking harmony with the infinite.

10. Be not a cancer on the earth-leave room for nature-leave room for nature.

While some have hailed the stones as a call to rational thinking, others have dubbed them the ten commandments of the Antichrist. There are many theories as to who is responsible for their existence, which include a long list of secret societies that are considered to be connected to the elite world group known as the Illuminati. However, there has been no further knowledge gained in the thirty-two years that they have been standing.

No one has come forward to take credit for the work, and no one has been found to offer an explanation. While the entire exhibit screams new world order, the most disturbing inscription is the call for maintaining humanity under five hundred million. Considering that there are more than 7 billion people on the earth today, this would seem to be a call for the extermination of more than 6.5 billion people. As we know according to scripture, there will be wars in the last days that decimate the earth's population, and it is likely that these wars will be orchestrated by the world's elite. Who have the mind-set of these guidelines that are written in stone.

At the Touch of a Button

With the advancement of technology, we have a common misconception that we have come a long way in the last several decades. There is no doubt that top secret government technology is mind blowing, and if you can dream it up, they have probably had it for the last twenty years. But what about the general public? Just how far have we come, and what are the advantages of our technology?

When you think about it, the advantages are few, and the cost is quite high. With the added expenses of cell phones, satellite TV, Internet, gaming systems, and online shopping, a large majority of the population has found themselves on the brink of bankruptcy. Considering the state of the economy, it seems as though we are staring into a black hole. And even our government is on the brink of bankruptcy.

As the middle class is disappearing and more and more people are finding themselves in poverty, we are still marching toward worldwide unification. The poor can receive free cell phones from the government, and anyone can access free Internet services from their local library. Staying connected to the world is not a problem, and with technology today, we can do nearly anything that can be imagined. And our society today has become very reminiscent of the first world empire and the tower of Babel, spoken of in the book of Genesis.

> And the Lord said, Behold, the people
> is one, and they have all one language;
> and this they begin to do: and now
> nothing will be restrained from them,
> which they have imagined to do.
> (Genesis 11:6)

The simple fact that we decided to walk on the moon, and it came to pass, really says it all. And that was nearly fifty years ago. Since that time unimaginable feats have not only become imaginable, but they have become a part of history. And if we consider the realm of entertainment, we have certainly witnessed every evil imagination of the heart come to life, through the works of special effects and computer generation.

With our daily dependence on technology increasing, we will be considered cave men in a few generations. What is most disturbing is the fact that a sudden loss of modern technology will leave those who have not lived without it in a clueless state of helplessness. What will such people do when a constant stream of media and entertainment are cut off? What will they eat when stores and restaurants are out of food or closed? As we grow closer to having everything at the touch of a button, the question is this, what will happen when the button doesn't work anymore?

The bad thing about easy living in a world of technology is the fact that many do not give God credit for our freedoms and luxuries. What is frightful is that so many references in the scriptures of ancient judgments were the result of our modern day activities. And the only difference between us is the fact that we have had thousands of years to learn from their mistakes.

> Behold, this was the iniquity of thy
> sister Sodom, pride, fulness of bread,
> and abundance of idleness was in her
> and in her daughters, neither did she
> strengthen the hand of the poor and
> needy. And they were haughty, and
> committed abomination before me:
> therefore I took them away as I saw
> good. (Ezekiel 16:49–50)

6

The Manifestation of Demons on Earth

For decades now, there have been countless horror films that have portrayed demonic creatures invading the earth. In various scenarios such as invasions from subterranean caverns, outer space, and from hell itself, we have had numerous visuals of what a frightening environment it would be. But has such entertainment brought us to the conclusion that it is a scenario only to be found in the movies? And at the same time, has it conditioned us to such horrific visualizations?

As the Bible foretells, there will in fact be hordes of demonic creatures that plague the inhabitants of the earth in the last days. My countless hours of study on the subject have answered many of my questions, and likely some of your own as well such as "Will a human being be able to kill them?" "Will they be in spirit form, or will they have physical bodies?" "What supernatural powers will they possess?"

Before we discern the prophetic description of the demonic creatures, let us first look at some examples and results of their nature—examples that can be found today, both in reality and entertainment. We will also find that sometimes reality is far more terrifying than fiction.

Signs of Their Coming

On May 26, 2012, police in St. Petersburg, Florida, responded to a call that was almost too horrific to be real.[1] It was regarding a man who was naked on the side of the street and appeared to be eating another human being. When police arrived on the scene, they immediately found themselves in the middle of a real-life horror film scenario. The naked man was in fact biting off another man's face, while the victim lay helpless beneath him.

The officer fired several shots into the attacker, and yet he continued to chew away on the victim, like a blood-thirsty beast or a zombie back from the dead. After a total of six rounds, the suspect collapsed and died. The condition of the victim was critical as he had lost much of his face, including his eyeballs. The attacker had apparently been taking illegal narcotics, which he had a history of, and the result of the attack was attributed to his drug use.

There have been numerous other incidents that are similar in nature. Police in a number of different states have recently had disturbing encounters with perpetrators who have been taken over by mind-altering drugs. Some of these incidents included suspects who were biting and violently attacking others. One such suspect was surrounded by officers who had drawn their firearms, and his only response was that of a wild and vicious animal, as he growled at them in a threatening manner.

There was a similar incident in early 2012 which involved my parents, who live in a country setting outside of Wright City, Missouri. A neighbor who lived up the hill and through the woods had been doing bath salts, a new homemade drug that is a cheap alternative to cocaine. The middle-aged man, and an ex con, had been thrust into a nightmarish reality when the drug had taken hold of him. He began his rampage by shooting his shotgun inside of his home and later stated that there were snakes all over the floor.

After he left his residence, he approached the homes of several neighbors, insisting that they let him in. When he made it down to my parents' home, he continued to do the same, insisting that they let him in, as he banged on the door of their home with his shotgun. He insisted that they were after him and were going to kill him. But he wouldn't say who. My parents felt sorry for him, as it was obvious that he was terrified. But for their own safety, they remained behind the locked door. After leaving my parents' home, he broke into a window of their neighbor's home across the street. It was at this time that the sheriff's department arrived. Just before he was restrained, his shotgun discharged its final shell, but no one was injured.

Another bizarre incident, in Rusk county Texas,[2] involved two parents who insisted that their baby was demon possessed. They sought help from a priest and requested that an exorcism be performed. Before any evaluation could be made concerning their claims, they took matters into their own hands and murdered their baby. The baby's body was found with more than fifteen bite marks; it had been bludgeoned with a hammer and had also been sexually assaulted.

A similar incident occurred with another couple who killed their three children, whom they claimed were demon possessed. [3] This case involved a three -year-old, a one-year-old, and a two-month-old infant. All three of the children's bodies were found with multiple stab wounds; they were decapitated and had also been sexually assaulted.

With such unthinkable crimes taking place as a result of the use of narcotics, is it not obvious that the use of such substances are an invitation to demons? And considering the circumstances of the crimes, we seem to have proof that demons are not only influencing the users but are now completely taking over the body, as though it were a vehicle of destruction.

There have always been powerful drugs that have horrible effects on the human mind. But never before have we witnessed such horrific outcomes of their use. Could it be a combination of narcotics and demonic entertainment that bring about such gory acts? We know that these crimes are a visual example of what we can expect to see when the demons literally arrive. And not only will the demonic creatures create a nightmarish reality, but these crimes are a sign of how people will behave when they are in the grip of terror. And that within itself is scary enough, is it not?

When the Pit Opens Up

In the book of Revelation, we read of a horrifying event that will befall humanity in the last days. During the sounding of the seven trumpets, we see a series of events that involve stars falling to the earth. When the first angel sounds his trumpet, hail and fire mingled with blood is cast upon the earth. And one-third of the trees are burnt up, and all green grass is burnt up. When the second angel sounds, a great burning mountain is cast into the sea, and one-third of the creatures in the sea die.

When the third angels sounds, a great star from heaven burning like a lamp falls upon one- third of the rivers and fountains of waters. And many men die because the waters are made bitter. When the fourth angel sounds, a third part of the sun is darkened and a third part of the moon and stars are darkened. And a third of the day was darkened, and a third of the night was darkened.

It is after these trumpets that an angel flying through the midst of heaven is heard proclaiming, "Woe, woe, woe," to the inhabiters of the earth by reason of the other voices of the trumpet of the three angels, which are yet to sound! And when the fifth angel sounds, a star falls from heaven to the earth, and to him is given the key of the bottomless pit. Now, there are two ways that we can interpret this event. One would be that this is another falling star that crashes on the earth. The second interpretation would be that this is a fallen angel that opens the bottomless pit.

If we consider the first possible interpretation, this would be the description of a meteor falling to the earth. Upon impact, it could trigger major earthquakes in key places, which could open up the bottomless pit. The second possible interpretation would involve an angel who is cast out of heaven to the earth, because the description of his descent is that he falls. This would likely be the accurate interpretation of this event. Because a star was described as falling to the earth in the sounding of the third trumpet also, but it was not described as a he but an it.

After the angel with the key opens the bottomless pit, there arises a smoke out of the pit, as the smoke of a great furnace. And the sun and the air are darkened by reason of the smoke of the pit. It is then that out of this smoke appear demonic creatures, which John called locusts. However, his likening them to locusts must be for the fact that there are hordes of them, because his description of their appearance is not that of locusts. And to them was given power to hurt men as the scorpions of the earth have power. But they were not to kill men.

> And the shapes of the locusts were like unto horses prepared unto battle; and on their heads were as it were crowns like gold, and their faces were as the faces of men. And they had hair as the hair of women, and their teeth were as the teeth of lions. And they had breastplates, as it were breastplates of iron; and the sound of their wings was as the sound of chariots of many horses running to battle. And they had tails like unto scorpions, and there were stings in their tails: and their power was to hurt men five months. (Revelation 9:7–10)

As we can see, John has given us anything but the description of locusts. But what are they? They seem to fit the description of mythological creatures such as centaurs and other creatures that are depicted in ancient art and sculptures. But what inspired ancient artists to create sculptures that depict such strange creatures? Did they actually exist and cohabit our world in ancient times? Let us consider the origin of demons and the time before the flood.

> And it came to pass, when men began to multiply on the face of the earth, and daughters were born unto them, That the sons of God saw the daughters of men that they were fair; and they took

> them wives of all which they chose. There
> were giants in the earth in those days, and
> also after that, when the sons of God came
> in unto the daughters of men, and they
> bare children to them, the same became
> mighty men which were of old, men of
> Renown. (Genesis 6:1, 2, 4)

It is likely that these mighty men of old, these men of renown, are pagan gods, which were the hybrid children of the sons of God, whom defiled themselves with the daughters of men. In the book of Enoch, we learn that the sons of God are fallen angels, who descended in the days of Jared. This time frame suggests that these beings cohabited the earth with mankind for more than a thousand years.

During their time on earth, the Nephilim, who were the offspring of the angels and the daughters of men, were abominable blood -thirsty beings. The book of Enoch describes the many abominations that they committed, such as cannibalism, the drinking of blood, and how they defiled themselves with the beasts of the field and the fowl of the air. This information would suggest genetic manipulation, which could have created a vast amount of bizarre creatures, such as beasts with human heads and vice versa. This could also have been the creation of the dinosaurs and would explain why God allowed them to perish in the flood.

When Enoch made known to the fallen angels what God had determined to do to the earth and all living flesh, which included their beloved offspring, they sought forgiveness. However, it was not granted, and God determined that they would be bound and that the souls of their offspring would remain in the earth. Thus was the evolution of evil spirits or demons.

The Return of the Fallen Angels

Immediately after the sounding of the fifth trumpet, and the hordes of locusts are released from the bottomless pit. We read of an even greater judgment. At the sounding of the sixth trumpet, a voice from the four horns of the golden altar which is before God says: "Loose the four angels which are bound in the great river Euphrates."

> And the four angels were loosed, which
> were prepared for an hour, and a day, and
> a month, and a year, for to slay the third
> part of men. And the number of the army
> of the horsemen were two hundred
> thousand thousand: and I heard the
> number of them. (Revelation 9:15–16)

The account of the fallen angels' descent, which is found in the book of Enoch, states that the number of fallen angels were two hundred. However, the book of Genesis suggests that there were other incidents of angels having fallen after that time (Ge. 6:4). There is no question as to whether or not these are fallen angels that are to be loosed, because if they were not evil, they would not be bound beneath a river. However, the identity of the angels is a mystery.

Just as much of a mystery is the identity of the two hundred million horsemen, which are directly connected to the four angels that are loosed, it has long been a doctrine that the interpretation of this army is a human army. And countries such as China have come into question because they could likely produce such a large number of soldiers. But there are too many holes in the theory of this being a human army, as we will review.

First, the only reason that anyone would suppose that this is a human army is because of only one word in the verse, which is *horsemen*. But John has also described the demonic creatures as locusts, which had the appearance of horses. So this does not literally suggest that these are men.

A common theory to explain the recurring instances of horsemen is that end-time battles will be fought on horseback, due to some malfunction or loss of modern equipment. However, this theory proves nothing, because John does not describe horses as we know them. Unless I am unaware of a species of horse that have the heads of lions and that issue fire from their mouths. This description in the following verse renders that theory useless.

> And thus I saw the horses in the vision,
>
> and them that sat on them, having

breastplates of fire, and of jacinth, and
brimstone: and the heads of the horses
were as the heads of lions; and out of
their mouths issued fire and smoke and
brimstone. (Revelation 9:17)

In this verse, we also see a description of the horsemen, which have breastplates of fire, and jacinth (which is a deep blue color) and brimstone. This is not a description of human armor anywhere on earth. And this is the only description that we have regarding the horsemen, at least in the book of Revelation. In search of deeper insight, I came across what is commonly thought to be a description of the locusts that come out of the pit in the book of Joel. However, after comparing the description to both the locusts and the two hundred million horsemen, they are much more comparable to the latter.

Let us review these verses and determine if they are speaking of the same beings.

Both visions are of the last days.

Blow ye the trumpet in Zion, and sound
an alarm in my holy mountain: let all the
inhabitants of the land tremble: for the
day of the Lord cometh, for it is nigh at
hand. (Joel 2:1)

Both visions describe an army.

They shall run like mighty men; they shall climb the wall like men of war; and they shall march every one on his ways, and they shall not break their ranks. (Joel 2:7)
And the number of the army of the horsemen were two hundred thousand thousand: and I heard the number of them. (Revelation 9:16)

Both destroy with fire before and behind.

A fire devoureth before them; and behind them a flame burneth: the land is as the garden of Eden before them, and behind them a desolate wilderness; yea, and nothing shall escape them. (Joel 2:3)
By these three was the third part of men killed, by the fire, and by the smoke, and by the brimstone, which issued out of their mouths. For their power is in their mouth, and in their tails: for their tails were like unto serpents, and had heads, and with them they do hurt. (Revelation 9:18–19)

Both visions are of a supernatural army.

Neither shall one thrust another; they shall walk every one in his path: and when they

> fall upon the sword, they shall not be
> wounded. They shall run to and fro in the
> city; they shall run upon the wall, they shall
> climb up upon the houses; they shall enter in
> at the windows like a thief. (Joel 2:8–9)
>
> And thus I saw the horses in the vision, and
> them that sat on them, having breastplates
> of fire, and of jacinth, and brimstone.
> (Revelation 9:17)

Both events have a worldwide effect.

> The earth shall quake before them; the
> heavens shall tremble: the sun and the
> moon shall be dark, and the stars shall
> withdraw their shining. (Joel 2:10)
>
> And the four angels were loosed, which
> were prepared for an hour, and a day,
> and a month, and a year, for to slay the
> third part of men. (Revelation 9:15)

So we see that the description of this army in the book of Joel is quite similar to the description of the army that John saw. It is also evident that these are not the descriptions of human soldiers, so what are they? They cannot be human because we read that there have never been the likes of them on the earth, nor will ever be again (Joel 2:2).

If we continue to read in the book of Revelation, the next significant event to befall humanity is when Satan and his angels are cast out of heaven. Could this event be related to the two hundred million horsemen who slay one third of mankind? Could these horsemen be the angels who are cast out to the earth with Satan?

> And the great dragon was cast out, that
> old serpent, called the Devil, and Satan,
> which deceiveth the whole world: he
> was cast out into the earth, and his
> angels were cast out with him.
> (Revelation 12:9)

According to Revelation 12:4, Satan cast the third part of the stars of heaven to the earth. The common interpretation of this is that these stars are the angels who fall with him. But why is there no mention of them, except that they are cast to the earth? If this many fallen angels are in the earth, there has to be serious consequences.

The next event that John describes immediately after the fall of Satan and his angels is the rise of the beast kingdom. This is very interesting because it would seem that these fallen angels play a role in this last kingdom, which will rule the earth, as in the days of the fallen angels prior to the flood. Let us consider what Jesus said regarding the last days and also what Daniel said regarding the fourth beast, which would be the last kingdom to rule.

Jesus describes the last days.

But as the days of Noah were, so shall also the coming of the Son of man be. (Matthew 24:37)

Daniel describes the beast kingdom.

And as the toes of the feet were part of iron, and part of clay, so the kingdom shall be partly strong, and partly broken. And whereas thou sawest iron mixed with miry clay, *they shall mingle themselves with the seed of men*: but they shall not cleave one to another, even as iron is not mixed with clay. (Dan.2:42–43,

italics mine)

In Daniel's description of the beast kingdom, he has made a very curious statement regarding the iron that is mixed with clay. It would seem as though he is describing two different types of beings that rule in this kingdom. We know that if there are going to be fallen angels in the earth, when Satan and his angels are cast out of heaven, it is likely that they will wreak the same havoc as the fallen angels did before the flood.

Everything seems to come full circle, and history repeats itself. The judgment of the flood was brought on by the corruption of the angels when they mingled themselves with the daughters of men (the seed of men) and created an abominable offspring. The earth was full of violence in those days, and the hearts of men were continually evil. And this is the exact description of what the last days will be like as well.

We have to assume that these angels who rebel and submit to Satan will rule with him when they are cast to the earth. To assume that they have no role to play in this end-time kingdom and that the entire world will be ruled by the Antichrist who is merely one man possessed by the devil would be absurd.

Another sign of history repeating itself is the prophecy of the two witnesses. These two men will prophesy in the last days for a thousand two hundred and threescore days (Re.11:30) . And after that, they shall be killed. One of these men we know to be Elijah because he was taken up to heaven and reserved for the last days. We also read the following verse concerning him in the book of Malachi.

> Behold, I will send you Elijah the prophet
> before the coming of the great and dreadful
> day of the Lord. (Malachi 4:5)

The only other man mentioned as having been taken up and preserved alive in the scriptures (unless we consider

Ezra in the Apocrypha) is Enoch. And we read the following concerning his preservation in the book of Genesis.

> And all the days of Enoch were three hundred sixty and five years: and Enoch walked with God: and he was not; for God took him. (Genesis 5:23–24)

Enoch was on earth during the days of the fallen angels and their offspring. He prophesied against them and informed them of the judgment that God had determined. It is very fitting that he will be one of the two witnesses to prophesy during the last days when the angels are in the earth again as they were before. Another reason to believe that he is one of the two witnesses is the fact that he was made aware of the events that would take place in the last days, as it is written in the epistle of Jude.

> And Enoch also, the seventh from Adam, prophesied of these, saying, behold, the Lord cometh with ten thousands of his saints, to execute judgment upon all, and to convince all that are ungodly among them of all their ungodly deeds which they have ungodly committed, and of all their hard speeches which ungodly sinners have spoken against him.
> (Jude 1:14–15)

The Greatest Horror on Earth

Though it would seem that the invasion of demons and the release of fallen angels would be fearful enough, it is only a preview of the horrors to come. When Satan is cast out of heaven, an angel proclaims: "Woe to the inhabitants of the earth and of the sea! For the devil is come down unto you, having great wrath, because he knoweth that he hath but a short time." It is after this event that we read of the kingdom of the beast, during which time the saints will be persecuted.

However, the worst is still yet to come, for we know that the wrath of the devil pales in comparison to the wrath of God. Those who fear God and obey his commands will suffer the wrath of the devil, while those who fear the devil and submit to his mark of the beast system will suffer the wrath of God. And the wrath of God is described in the seven vial judgments, which will affect all those who have submitted to the beast.

> And I heard a voice out of the temple
> saying to the seven angels, Go your
> ways, and pour out the vials of the
> wrath of God upon the earth. And the
> first went, and poured out his vial
> upon the earth; and there fell a
> noisome and grievous sore upon the
> men which had the mark of the beast,
> and upon them which worshipped his
> image. (Revelation 16:1–2)

This judgment, the first of the seven vial judgments, seems to only affect those who have submitted to the beast. The theory of this mark of the beast being in the form of an implantable microchip would seem to gain credibility from this description. If there is a system in place that requires all people to have these implants, there could likely be a biological agent inside of the chip, which could release a virus inside the person in which it is implanted. It could also be that there will be some form of malfunction in the implants, which would possibly cause sores.

> And the second angel poured out his vial upon the sea; and it became as the blood of a dead man: and every living soul died in the sea. And the third angel poured out his vial upon the rivers and fountains of waters; and they became blood. (Revelation 16:3–4)

At this point, there will be no more water in the earth but only blood. The human body cannot survive for more than several days without water. So unless there are vast amounts of water reserves that have not been turned to blood, these judgments are occurring in rapid succession and only a few days from the end. Still it gets worse. Because there is nothing like a lack of drinking water, except a lack of drinking water on a really hot day.

> And the fourth angel poured out his vial
> upon the sun; and power was given unto him
> to scorch men with fire. And men were
> scorched with great heat, and blasphemed
> the name of God. (Revelation 16:8–9)

The description of this judgment is found in the book of Isaiah and is quite unique from other descriptions of the last days. During the trumpet judgments, we read the description of the sun being darkened and numerous prophets have also described the same. Let us look at a few of the descriptions as they were given by the prophets.

* *Isaiah:* "The darkness shall cover the earth, and gross darkness the people" (Is. 60:2).
* *Amos:* "The day of the lord is darkness, and not light" (Amos 5:1).
* *Joel:* "A day of darkness and gloominess, a day of clouds and of thick darkness" (Joel 2:2).
* "The sun and the moon shall be darkened, and the stars shall withdraw their Shining" (Joel 3:15).
* *Zephaniah:* "A day of darkness and gloominess, a day of clouds and thick darkness" (Ze. 1:15).

We have a description concerning the last days that seems to repeat itself. However, we have a verse in the book of Isaiah that describes the exact opposite and suggests that it will in fact be very bright and very hot. I believe that in this verse, Isaiah is describing the effects of the vial that is poured out by the fourth angel in the book of Revelation 16:8–9.

> Moreover the light of the moon shall be as
> the light of the sun, and the light of the sun
> shall be sevenfold, as the light of seven days,
> in the day that the Lord bindeth up the
> breach of his people, and healeth the stroke
> of their wound. (Isaiah 30:26)

After this, we read that the fifth angel pours out his vial upon the seat of the beast, and the kingdom of the beast becomes full of darkness. And when the sixth angel pours out his vial upon the great river Euphrates (*which must be blood at this point*), it is dried up, which prepares the way of the kings of the east. This is when all are gathered together unto the battle of Armageddon. It is after this that the seventh angel pours out his vial into the air and a great voice from the temple in heaven proclaims: "It is done."

Concerning the battle of Armageddon, we have numerous verses that give us a description of not only what it will be like but also the amount of people that will be killed in it. While we know it to be the valley of Armageddon in the book of Revelation, elsewhere in the old Testament it is referred to as the valley of decision.

> Put ye in the sickle, for the harvest is ripe: come, get you down; for the press is full, the fats overflow; for their wickedness is great. Multitudes, multitudes in the valley of decision: for the day of the Lord is near in the valley of decision. (Joel 3:13–14)
>
> And the angel thrust in his sickle into the earth, and gathered the vine of the earth, and cast it into the great winepress of the wrath of God. (Revelation 14:19)

The next verse in the book of Revelation tells us a lot regarding the outcome of this event. John not only gives us a description of the horror he has seen in his vision, but he gives us measurements that we can break down for a close estimation of the body count.

> And the winepress was trodden without the city, and blood came out of the winepress, even unto the horse bridles, by the space of a thousand and six hundred furlongs. (Revelation 14:20)

According to the chart of Jewish weights and measures in the works of Josephus (the Jewish historian who lived during the time of John), I found that a furlong is equivalent to 700 feet. Therefore, when John says 1,600 furlongs, it is the equivalent of 1,120,000 feet. This number of square footage is equivalent to approximately 25.7 acres. The height of the average horse is between five and six feet tall; therefore, the bridle would be between five and six feet off the ground.

The average amount of blood that is in the human body is approximately 10 pints/5 liters or 1.3 gallons. An Olympic-size swimming pool holds 660,252 gallons of water, and it would take seventy-five Olympic-size pools to fill 25.7 acres. Therefore, it would take an absolute minimum of 37,489,875 people to produce the amount of blood that John saw in his vision. This would be assuming that every drop of blood has been drained from each and every body and that is quite unlikely. Considering this, the number of bodies that produced this amount of blood is almost certainly much higher.

After the seventh angel pours out his vial and the voice from the temple in heaven proclaims "It is done," there is a great earthquake. Such as was not since men were upon the earth so mighty an earthquake and so great. Thus are the judgments of God in the days when the seven angels pour out the vials of the wrath of God upon the earth. And there shall be a new heaven and a new earth, for the first heaven and the first earth will pass away. And only judgment shall remain.

> And I saw a great white throne, and him
> that sat on it, from whose face the earth
> and the heaven fled away; and there was

found no place for them. And I saw the dead, small and great, stand before God; and the books were opened: and another book was opened, which is the book of life: and the dead were judged out of those things which were written in the books, according to their works.
(Revelation 20:11–12)

In the following verse from the Apocrypha, we see a clear description of the judgment. It will be stern, there will be no compassion, everyone will be judged according to their works, and no one shall escape it.

> And the most high shall be revealed upon the seat of judgment, and compassion shall pass away, and patience shall be withdrawn; but only judgment shall remain, truth shall stand, and faithfulness shall grow strong.
> (2 Esdras 7:33–34)

7

What Will Become of the Church?

For two thousand years, we have witnessed the global expansion of today's largest religion, Christianity. With an estimated 2.18 billion Christians worldwide and more than 40,000 denominations and organizations, it is hard to comprehend that a world leader will one day subdue such large numbers. Considering that Christians make up nearly one -third of the global population and yet we are told that the whole world will wonder after the beast, there has to be serious changes coming concerning the church.

To Be Closed Or Converted?

In the United States alone, there are approximately 246,780,000 people that identify themselves as being Christian. And with an estimated 350,000 churches throughout the country, it is hard to imagine that they will eventually be desolate. But what will become of them? Will they be vacant dusty structures filled with cobwebs, like the buildings that are depicted in an apocalyptic film? Or will they be thriving places of worship for those who submit to the beast?

Scripture would seem to suggest the latter as would modern statistics regarding the faith. Of the estimated 80 percent of the United States population who say that they are Christians, recent survey polls reveal that only 20 to 30 percent actually attend a church. This information could explain how so many people will be deceived in the last days. If the other 50 or 60 percent of stay at home Christians are not doing studies at home, they could one day walk into a "church of the Antichrist" and not even know the difference.

Regarding the signs of the end, Jesus said that the gospel must first be published among all nations (Mk. 13:10) . And Paul said in his epistle to the Thessalonians that there must also be a falling away first (2 Thess. 2:3). The Greek word for *falling* is *apostasia*, which means defection from the truth "apostasy," to fall away or to forsake. This has already begun and will likely be the reason that so many will be deceived.

With more than 1,500 different faith groups currently active in North America, there is no doubt that many of them have false doctrines. Some of these denominations hold such strange doctrines that it is obvious they do not know the Bible. With large numbers of Christian members who subscribe to such unscriptural doctrines, they have already been led astray. When the false prophet and the Antichrist begin their campaign, such Christians will follow due to their lack of knowledge concerning the word of God.

During the second half of the tribulation, the false prophet will institute the mark of the beast system. It will be during this time that all mankind shall be made to worship the beast or be killed. It is most likely that by this time the rapture of the church has already taken place. Therefore, all that remains of the church will be those who have identified themselves as Christians and have done nothing more than simply that.

Considering the atmosphere at this time point, with plagues, natural disasters, and wars, many people will likely find themselves seeking comfort from a church. But the question is this, how far removed will the truth be at this time? Furthermore, will they be able to tell the difference? If the whole world is caused to worship the beast, there will undoubtedly be more than just a false prophet making this happen.

We are warned in the scriptures to see that we are not deceived, and we are told that a great deception will come. Therefore it is most likely that there will be countless ministers and churches that fall for the deception. We can say with certainty that there will not be authentic churches as we know them during this time. Because without the mark of the beast, it would be impossible for a church to be in operation. And true Christians will certainly not have this mark.

Concerning the great deception and the false prophet, there has long been a theory that there will be a defective pope at the time of the end. Nostradamus predicted that this would come to pass in the last days, and many people believe it to be a likely scenario. Considering that the pope is viewed as a deity by Catholics and the fact that Catholics make up more than one billion of the 2.18 billion Christian population, that would indeed be a great deception. And if a deity such as the pope were to approve the mark of the beast to the billion Catholics that depend on him for guidance and instruction, this would be the damnation of half the Christians in the world.

The Vatican has already publicly announced that any denomination outside of Catholicism is not a legitimate church. In the event of a pope declaring that Christians should take the mark of the beast, all Christians who know the truth and refuse the mark of the beast will be labeled among the illegitimate denominations. If this scenario were to actually come to pass, all denominations outside of Catholicism would likely be condemned by the pope. All such denominations would be labeled as cults and dangerous fanatics. And if Christians refuse to take the mark of the beast, they will be labeled as terrorists, who belong to anti-government terrorist organizations.

The Congregation Become the Ministers

Those who remain after the rapture that have a Christian background will fit into one of two categories—those who allow themselves to be deceived and those who know the truth, and those who know the truth will suffer regret for not having embraced a sinless life before the rapture. They will also suffer persecution and ultimately execution for keeping their faith and obeying God.

Aside from simply trying to evade evil authorities, those who know the truth will also be responsible for warning others not to take the mark. In the book of Daniel, we read interesting verses regarding the time of the Antichrist. They give us a good description of those who are left after the rapture.

> And they that understand among the
> people shall instruct many: yet they
> shall fall by the sword, and by flame,
> by captivity, and by spoil, many days.
> And some of them of understanding
> shall fall, to try them, and to purge,
> and to make them white, even to the
> time of the end: because it is yet for a
> time appointed. (Daniel 11:33, 350

So, many will in fact know the truth and will inform and save others from the mark of damnation. However, we also read that many will be taken into captivity and will die by the sword and by flame and by spoil. Though there will be great risk and great tribulation, there will still be people instructing others and sharing the testimony of Jesus Christ. And their reward will certainly be great for their efforts.

One could say that preaching the gospel in the last days will be comparable to the preaching of the gospel in the time of its beginning. It was a bold new covenant, and many were severely persecuted for it. Today, there are an average of 159,960 Christians who are martyred for their faith each year. As large as this number is, however, it will surely pale in comparison to the number of martyrs in the last days.

Those who will preach in the last days will not do so in a church, because this will not be allowed. Rather, as in the days of Jesus and his disciples, they will roam to and fro sharing the gospel. And just as in the days of Jesus, they will likely carry nothing with them, and yet God will make a way for them.

Christians that are left after the rapture will have the unique opportunity of saving the last of the living. It will also be the most challenging time to call sinners to repentance. While salvation is free and easily obtainable now, many do not repent. During the tribulation, convincing sinners to repent will require their life, and instructing them not to take the mark will cause them to break the law.

To be left after the rapture and to suffer the great tribulation, it will be amazing enough to obtain personal redemption. But to be left behind and bring many lost people into the kingdom of God, that will be astounding. And it is likely that many who know the truth will not be taken in the rapture for that purpose alone.

Apocalyptic Survival

When the time comes and the end is evident, survival will be crucial for those who need to save the lost. Aside from the human threat, which will be the evil ruling government and those who would inform them, there will also be the supernatural threat—all the plagues also, the earthquakes, the wars, and the famines. Evasion and survival will be nearly impossible. As the saying goes, "Only the strong survive," but what is the definition of strong in a situation such as this?

There are a growing number of people who are preparing for doomsday and the worst case scenario. They include individual survivalists, teams, small groups, and even large families. The focus of their preparations typically involve three main issues. The first is location. Most of these groups and families have a designated retreat to gather at in the event of an emergency. These retreats usually consist of an isolated area, with a secure dwelling place such as an underground bunker or well hidden shelter.

The second issue of focus is food and water supply. The focus on food storage is likely the one issue that every survivalist and prepper is concerned with. Many of those who prepare have large quantities of dry food that can be stored for extended periods. Some families have shared a glimpse of their preparatory efforts on reality shows. They have displayed pantries and basements that are choked with boxes of food. They confess that they are well prepared for any scenario and are boastful that they are one step ahead of society.

Their major problem however is that they live in large communities in suburban areas that are choked with many houses and many people. In the event of a major crisis, they would not last beyond a few days without having mobs of hungry people knocking at their door. When this happens, they will have to make one of two choices. The first choice would be to accommodate their neighbors and share their supplies. In making this decision, the result would be devastating to their food count and would drastically diminish their estimated time of survival.

The second choice that they could make would be to refuse those who are hungry. In making this decision, they would be forced to defend themselves and their home. This could create an all out slaughter and the destruction of their home. Ultimately in either decision, they will come to the realization that they have stored large quantities of food for other people to end up eating. And they will find themselves just as vulnerable as those around them who made no preparations whatsoever.

The third issue of focus is weaponry and combative training. Many people have stockpiled rifles and ammunition for self- defense. Preparations of both the location and food are made in vain without this issue. If you have land for an emergency retreat, you should have the means to defend it. The same can be said for food storage. In the event of a crisis that shuts down food distribution or in the event of hyperinflation, you would literally be sitting on a pile of gold.

So how well would these common preparations pay off in a serious crisis? If the crisis were short-lived, it is likely that such preparations would be the difference between life and death. But what about an actual doomsday scenario, such as the seven-year tribulation? Let us consider the outcome of each of these preparations if they were made in the anticipation of the tribulation. With prophetic verses in the Bible that give us a depiction of the last days, we can determine whether or not certain preparations would be in vain.

The issue regarding location is crucial for any major crisis. In the event of a disaster, which could include riots and civil unrest, or in the event of an invasion by a foreign army, the best place to be is as far away from the masses as possible. However, if the goal is simply to survive for the sake of surviving, it won't matter where you are. If God is calling you out for repentance or to complete a task such as helping others come to repentance, you will not be safe anywhere. There are multiple verses that depict the outcome for those who will hide themselves in the last days. This would include all places that one could retreat.

> Though they dig into hell, thence shall mine hand take them; though they climb up to heaven, thence will I bring them down: And though they hide themselves in the top of Carmel, I will search and take them out thence; and though they be hid from my sight in the bottom of the sea, thence will I command the serpent, and he shall bite them. (Amos 9:2–3)
> And the kings of the earth, and the great men, and the rich men, and the chief captains, and the mighty men, and every bondman, and every free man, hid themselves in the dens and in the rocks of the mountains. (Revelation 6:15)

These verses clearly tell us that there will be no place that is safe to hide. While an isolated retreat or an underground bunker may save you from the threat of man, there will be no escape if you are hiding from God. Concerning the second issue which is food preparation, there is also no hope without the help of God. Concerning the tribulation of the last days, one would need a seven-year supply of food that would not go bad. And extreme weather or the threat of looting and thievery could change that in a moment's notice.

The odds of sustaining a good food source are much better if one has an isolated retreat. If one has land to grow their own food and harvest game such as deer, they will be far more likely to survive. However, the threat of severe weather could alter crop harvest, and there are no guarantees when hunting either. The third preparation, which includes weaponry, is somewhat comparable to the issue of a hiding place. It will only protect you from the threat of man, but we know that there will also be many supernatural threats to deal with as well.

Concerning the possession of firearms, much of the world already has strict laws in place. Many nations do not allow their citizens the right to bear arms, and when the world unites under the final empire, the United States will be no exception. It is only a matter of time before we witness a serious increase of strict gun laws. When the time comes, anyone who has a firearm will be labeled a terrorist threat.

There is of course the option of battling an oppressive government. But instances in the past, such as the events of Ruby ridge and Waco Texas, have proven that the government will go to any lengths to disarm citizens—even murdering innocent children. And the standoff between the federal government and the branch Davidians at their compound in Waco Texas was a clear example of what will happen in the last days.

Because the branch Davidians were considered an unorthodox cult and possessed a large quantity of firearms, many people found it easier to turn their heads and accept the slaughter of these people and their children. When the mark of the beast system draws near and the new government rule is established, mainstream Christians like you and me will be labeled the same as they were. We will be considered cult members, extremists, dangerous threats to society that must be taken out by the government. And the brainwashed masses will applaud them for doing so. We must also consider what scripture says regarding combative actions and self-defense.

> He that leadeth into captivity shall go
> into captivity: he that killeth with the
> sword must be killed with the sword.
> Here is the patience and the faith of
> the saints. (Revelation 13:10)

This verse would suggest an eye for an eye and a tooth for a tooth. But does it suggest that those who are defending themselves will come to the same end as those who are killing and taking captive? Much like the decision regarding the mark of the beast, the question of self-defense in the last days holds a mysterious answer. While it would seem only logical to save your life and accept the mark, we know that we cannot do so. Likewise, it would seem logical to defend yourself and your family by engaging in a firefight with an evil government that wants to mark or kill you and your family.

Jesus could have prevented his capture and crucifixion, but he did not do so. If Christians avoid captivity by engaging the enemy and taking human lives, this would certainly not be following the example of Jesus Christ. It would also be breaking one of the Ten Commandments. And after all is said and done, the end result is that you will be killed anyway. The only difference is whether or not you have blood on your hands when you die.

As for the supernatural threat, it would seem as though there will be no hope for self-defense. Concerning this prophecy in the book of Joel and his description of a supernatural army, we find that weapons will have no effect on them.

> Neither shall one thrust another; they
> shall walk every one in his path: and
> when they fall upon the sword, they
> shall not be wounded. (Joel 2:8)

Having studied the book of Joel and considered this verse in particular, I have answered a question that I have long since pondered. We know that we will be helpless in the events of earthquakes and serious weather and also powerless under the shadow of an evil government. Finally, there will be no means of combating the supernatural beings that are made manifest.

Perhaps the only use that we will get out of our dependence on firearms will be whatever we can hunt and kill with them for the sake of food. It would be nice to think that we would have a fighting chance with the right hardware, but according to scripture, it would only be a fantasy. And no matter how many guns we have, they will not alter the outcome of what will come to pass.

The dependence on man and the dependence on man-made weapons will certainly be in vain. The only hope for mankind is God. So we should focus our dependence upon him. When the time comes, God will be the only answer for those who were not taken in the rapture. And when you think about it, his purpose for those who remain would surely not be to engage in combat and kill those who do not understand.

Rather there will be an example to set for many lost people. The faith and knowledge of the eternal life that awaits will strengthen those who know the truth. Ultimately the only weapon that will prevail is the word of God. And the only survivors will be those who know and share the word of God. Of course, this means that those who are left will have to live off the grid. If the government will not allow commerce without the mark of the beast, then we know that those who resist will be considered a threat to the system and to society.

The time after the rapture will be the worst time in history. Many will have to rely on good people that have a substantial food source as an alternative to the mark of the beast. And many will likely starve to death as a result of declining the mark and also due to the famine that will have the whole world in its grip.

8

A Nightmare Becomes Reality

Through the special effects of modern entertainment, we have witnessed just about every possible worst case scenario befall mankind. What they all have in common is this, mankind always survives and the credit is given to man for saving the day rather than God. As worst case scenarios continue to play out in entertainment, the worst case scenarios are building up in reality. And mankind will have no chance of survival without the help of God himself.

As we step a little closer each day to the tribulation, we can see prophecy unfolding in current events. And there is no doubt that the world has already begun shaking. Another glimpse of the coming horrors has come to many people in the form of dreams and visions. Documented and shared with the public, there are many similar visions concerning the United States. Visions of a great famine, disasters, civil unrest, and civil war have all been seen as a result of fasting and praying.

Prophetic Dreams

Concerning dreams and visions, my wife and I have certainly had our share since coming to the Lord in 2011. My dreams began in late 2009 and consisted of recurring tornadoes. In each dream, there would be multiple tornadoes that surrounded me, and in the dreams, there was no hope for escape. As time has passed since having the last tornado dream in 2010, it has become obvious that this was a sign that a serious storm was coming in my life.

Not only a personal warning, but I believe that these dreams were also a vision of the 2011 tornado outbreak that began in the spring. Not only was it the worst tornado outbreak in recorded history, but it struck close to home. At one point during the outbreak, we were watching as a softball- sized hail pounded our vehicles through our back window. Little did we know that if we had been watching out our front window, we would have seen one of the tornadoes that had come within close proximity.

While we managed to make it through the violent storm season, the result of the oversized hail left us with more than ten thousand dollars in damages. However, concerning my dreams of surrounding tornadoes, our personal life was just entering a storm. As we were both working opposite shifts, my wife working days and myself working nights, I began to dream a different theme.

Now the recurring dreams had become more personal. And I was seeing images of myself, my wife, and our three children living back home with my parents. This made no sense to me, or to my wife. Considering that we had been living in the same house that we bought when we were only teenagers, we had no reason to move. We had purchased a large home in the anticipation of having multiple children. We were in a nice enough neighborhood, so the dreams just weren't adding up.

While the economy has been steadily going down hill since 2008 and many Americans have lost their homes, this did not seem to be the importance of the recurring dreams. The warning dreams involved a threat to us while living at my parent's residence. In multiple dreams, there was a deadly hunting accident that occurred. In other dreams of us living at my parents, there were armed trespassers that posed a serious threat.

In October of 2011, my wife lost her job due to attendance problems that resulted from health-related issues. While our concerns for paying the mortgage and other debts increased, it was still out of the question that we would lose our home. However, only two months later, I also lost my job due to attendance issues that resulted from health-related issues. Considering the strain on our income from my wife having lost her job and the fact that we had just paid for our children's Christmas, we suddenly found ourselves hopeless at the snap of a finger.

As a typical decision of a greedy corporation that only cares about the dollar, they terminated me only four days before I was to receive twelve hundred dollars in vacation pay. Considering that we were broke and low on groceries, that money that was due to me would have certainly came in handy, especially considering that it could have helped feed my children. But it was likely spent on alcohol for management. And I suppose they needed it, to be able to live with themselves considering their disgusting and selfish nature.

As you can imagine, after no luck finding work, in August of 2012, our home was foreclosed on. We were given a two-week notice to remove all our possessions that we had accumulated over twelve years of living in our home. And it was at that point that my dreams had manifested themselves into reality. And through prayer and fasting, the Lord made it clear to us that this was where he wanted us and that he had big plans in store for us.

Without God, it would have been very easy to slip into a depression, having lost everything we had worked so hard for, for so long. However, we were very optimistic and cheerful, considering that we were being guided by the Lord. When you know that you are doing the will of God, there is an indescribable peace. Even if you are in a bad situation that would otherwise leave you hopeless, you have peace knowing that God is in total control.

Concerning the warning dreams that involved a threat from armed and unknown trespassers, I had all but forgotten them considering all the things that were going on at the time. Having moved back in with my parents, my wife and I had a new optimism for finding work. We had lived over fifty miles and two counties away, and there were a lot more job opportunities for us living in their area. However, after submitting application after application, there seemed to be few places that were actually hiring.

With no prospects of finding work, we found ourselves waiting on a phone call that never came. With bow season opening in less than a month, I began scouting the woods of my parents' property to keep myself occupied. Knowing that we were where God wanted us to be was sufficient. And I was working on numerous books, writing for sometimes all hours of the day. Still, staying indoors was not an option for me. I couldn't allow myself to become depressed, so I anticipated the opening of the coming hunting season.

Considering the fact that my parents own less than four acres, I requested hunting permission from the owner of the land that connects to my parents' property. After contacting him over the phone, he granted me sole permission to hunt his twelve wooded acres, with the exception of my brother. Considering that he lived out of state and no one else had hunting permission, I had a better than average chance of harvesting a nice buck.

I had just started hunting in 2009, and I only had one rack to show for it. Having had no luck for the past two seasons, I was confident that all of that was about to change. In less than twenty-four hours of opening day for bow season, I took my first doe. And I even had a souvenir to show from it for my first deer taken with a bow. She had a wooden napkin ring holder on her right leg just above the hoof that she was wearing like a bracelet. My wife determined that it had apparently stepped into it outside nearby restaurant that is located in a wooded resort.

A few weeks after taking the doe, I finally found what I was looking for in a picture from my trail camera. At 7:00 a.m., standing less than thirty yards from my tree stand was a very nice ten-point buck. Just when I was ready to give up on seeing a nice buck in the area, I finally had proof that he was out there. And considering the lack of hunters in the immediate area, I was sure that I would get him.

However, only a few days after this, I received some disturbing news from the neighbor that lives on the other side of the property that I was given permission to hunt. He told me that some of his buddies had been illegally hunting the property for the past few years, and they too had become aware of this buck from the scouting they were doing while they were trespassing. Considering the fact that the property owner lived out of state, they viewed this area to be a free for all hunting spot.

The idea of this buck being taken illegally by trespassers made me sick. And the neighbor that informed me of them also told me that they would begin hunting the property when rifle season opened, which was less than two weeks away. With the advantage of being a bow hunter, when most of the hunters in the area only hunt with firearms, I knew that I still had a chance to take the buck, but time was running out.

On Saturday, October 27, I climbed into my tree stand and spoke to the Lord. I informed him of my dilemma. I told him that I was determined to take this buck before the trespassers could steal him, but this meant that I would have to put in a lot of hunting hours and miss church the next morning. I told the Lord, "If you will send that buck my way, I will be in church first thing in the morning giving you praise."

Less than five minutes passed after saying my prayer, and the very buck that I was after walked right out in front of me. I took him at twenty yards and began repeatedly thanking God. And as it turned out, he was actually an eleven-pointer. Not only was he the biggest deer I had ever taken but later in the season I took an even bigger one. It was a record size eight-pointer that landed me in the Pope and Young club. And needless to say, I was in church the next morning with a smile on my face.

When rifle season opened, I had encounters with several armed trespassers, all of whom acknowledged that they were breaking the law. Not only were they trespassing on the out-of-state landowner, but they had even made their way down onto my parents' property. As my warning dreams came into remembrance, my wife and I took a day to post private property and no trespassing signs in strategic places on the property lines. I truly believe that the actions we have taken and the extra precautionary measures that we have considered have prevented a possible tragic accident. And I thank God for the warning dreams that he gave me.

Concerning my wife's dreams, we have been given a much more profound vision of not only our own personal life but the future of our entire nation. The first among many prophetic dreams that she was given involved chaotic cosmic activity and a great earthquake. After this dream, which occurred in early 2012, we began to dream similar dreams that had very specific details regarding our future.

I was experiencing recurring dreams of fighter jets that literally covered the entire view of the sky. I also had been experiencing recurring dreams of us moving into a new house. As we began sharing our dreams on a regular basis, we discovered that we were both having dreams of the exact same house, which was the size of a mansion in description. This was hard to imagine considering that we were nearly bankrupt. But there was no doubt that the Lord was showing us these things as we continued to receive confirmation through prayer and fasting.

In one of her dreams of us living in this new house, she was also shown a large property that the house sat on. The property included crop fields as well as plenty of woodland. In her dream, she was shown strange aircraft that was flying over our property. It was not comparable to any aircraft that she had ever seen before. She did recognize however that it was being operated by the United States military as she saw a passenger looking out of it that was in a US military issue uniform.

After one of the aircraft landed nearby, our home was surrounded by military personnel, and they were pounding on the front door of our home. After opening the door, they came in and conducted a quick search. Afterward, I accompanied them to another room where they spoke to me in private for several minutes. When we came out of the room, I showed them to the door, and then they were gone.

After they left, she was sitting on our bed when I came to give her a strange message. I looked at her and said, "Watch out for the spiders." She then looked behind her to see if there was a spider on the bed.

She then asked, "What spiders? Do you see a spider?"

Again, I said, "Watch out for the spiders!"

She replied, "What spiders?"

When I answered for the last time, I said, "Beware of the black widows!"

When she woke up, she shared the dream with me, and we began discussing a possible interpretation. There was no doubt that it was a warning dream that regarded our future. One interesting detail of the dream was that a glimpse of our children gave her the impression that they were about three to five years older. After reviewing the dream for less than five minutes, I determined three key words that we could use for a Google search in hopes of finding answers. The key words were *military* and *black widows*.

To our amazement, we immediately found answers to the strange dream that she had just experienced. The mysterious black aircraft that were in her dream is also found in reality. The Black Widows are a combat aviation company of the United States army based in Ohio and Kentucky. They have a history that goes all the way back to World War II. Their motto is "Mate and kill," and they are also known as the spiders.

There has been plenty of talk over the years about "the black helicopters" flying over for such a scenario to not be taken seriously. If such things are repeatedly portrayed in film and on television as a myth, the public will automatically rule them out as a real possibility. If such scenarios have been burned into our subconscious as fiction, it will be hard to convince even ourselves of what is right before our very eyes.

The result of such a dream has made me seriously reconsider some of my work. It would make good sense that I could potentially one day receive a visit from special ops concerning some of the literature I have written about the one-world government agenda. However, we do not feel that we were a specific target of this campaign, as there were many aircraft flying over in the dream. It is likely that such an event will be broad and involve many citizens.

In a more recent dream involving the property that has been the center of past dreams, we received far more revelation than any other before it. This dream not only served as a warning dream but seemed to be an instructional dream as well. In this dream, my wife was lying in bed and looking at the moon through a skylight in the ceiling when three angels came into view. Two of the angels were on each side of the moon, one was wearing a red robe and the other was wearing a white robe.

The two angels seemed to take hold of the moon, and they pulled it back until it was no longer visible. It was then that the third angel came closer to the earth until it was standing right before my wife. The third angel was wearing a blue robe, and we have interpreted that the revelation of this dream specifically affects the United States because the angels were dressed in red, white, and blue.

She described a misty fog round about the angel, and it was then that she was shown crystal clear images. She saw vegetables and produce that were rotten, and she saw crops that were extremely undeveloped. After seeing these things, she was shown large groups of people who were fighting over food. And she was shown large cities that were filled with chaos due to people rioting and widespread civil unrest.

After these visions, she was given a view of our own personal property. She saw a large garden that covered several acres, a large green house, and hundreds of acres of healthy crops. The most interesting vision in this dream was a unique irrigation system that allowed us to have an abundance of crops to harvest at a time when the majority of crop fields were failing. This unique irrigation system was shown to her in detail and would no doubt pay off in the event of a severe drought.

When considering our prophetic dreams overall, there are two key points that are obvious in nearly each and every one of them. The first is that perilous times are approaching, and that our nation is going to experience suffering of biblical proportions. The second is that we are going to be in a situation where we can help a lot of people. It goes without saying that we will not be able to do such things without the help of God. So we have given our life over to the will of God so that such things can be accomplished through us.

When People Eat Their Own

Desperate times are on the way, and as the saying goes, "Desperate times call for desperate measures." But just how desperate will the measures be? If there were a severe famine next year, what would be the worst case scenario in terms of the desperate measures that some would take? It would no doubt be cannibalism. And in such dire situations, it is not only likely that people will eat the flesh of the recently deceased, but that there will be people who are killing others just for the sake of eating them.

Instances of cannibalism have surfaced in our modern world, as a result of life or death situations. A good example of this would be the events of the plane crash in the Andes in 1972.[1] As a result of the crash, and an avalanche that occurred thereafter, forty -five passengers had been quickly reduced to only eighteen survivors. As a result of having no food, a collective decision was soon made to eat the flesh of those who had perished among them. This decision was agreed upon for the sake of survival, even though the dead were close personal friends.

These survivors were not members of some bizarre tribe but were civilized people like any of us. They even identified themselves as Christians of the Roman Catholic faith. And yet for the sake of their own lives, they resorted to cannibalism. Let us take a look at the instances of cannibalism in the Bible. As we study the possibility of a great end-time famine that will cause desperate people to consider the unthinkable.

> And ye shall eat the flesh of your sons,
> and the flesh of your daughters shall
> ye eat. (Leviticus 26:29)

And as the king of Israel was passing by
upon the wall, there cried a woman unto
him, saying, Help, my lord, O king. And he
said, If the Lord do not help thee, whence
shall I help thee? Out of the barn-floor, or
out of the winepress? And the king said
unto her, What aileth thee? And she
answered, This woman said unto me, Give
thy son, that we may eat him to day, and
we will eat my son to morrow. So we
boiled my son, and did eat him: and I said
unto her on the next day, Give thy son, that
we may eat him: and she hath hid her son.
(2 Kings 6:26–29)

Therefore the fathers shall eat the sons in the
midst of thee, and the sons shall eat their
fathers; and I will execute judgments in thee,
and the whole remnant of thee will I scatter
into all the winds. (Ezekiel 5:10)

And I will cause them to eat the flesh of
their sons and the flesh of their daughters,
and they shall eat every one the flesh of
his friend in the siege and straitness,
wherewith their enemies, and they that
seek their lives, shall straiten them.
(Jeremiah 19:9)

With a great famine that will have global effects, the practice of cannibalism will likely be the most shocking evidence of it being a reality. Like anything else, it simply comes down to whether or not you trust in God. If there are people out there that have no faith, and we know there are many, they will not endure hunger while waiting on the Lord. And then there are the people who do not regard God at all. How quickly will they be reduced to subhuman eating machines when the basic survival instincts kick in?

The result of such a famine is perhaps the closest we will ever get to the common scenario of popular zombie films. The plot for any zombie film involves a small percentage of the population, fighting off hordes of mindless flesh eating corpses. While such films are the work and nonsense of Hollywood and only serve to corrupt the mind of the viewer, they could one day reflect reality.

In medical terms, the result of consuming human flesh has devastating effects that are similar to mad cow disease.[2] Known as CJD (Creutzfeldt-Jakob disease), the symptoms include the following: rapidly progressive dementia, memory loss, changes in personality, hallucinations, rigid posture, and seizures. These symptoms are said to be caused by the progressive death of the brain's nerve cells. If we consider the fact that there will be a time when men shall seek death but not find it (Re. 9:6), we could potentially have mindless zombies roaming the earth and eating the flesh of other human beings.

Another reason to consider such an epidemic as a possibility is the nature of God's judgments. It would be ignorant, to say the least, to assume that God approves of what we consider entertainment today. The vile nature of such zombie horror films, not to mention the excessive profanity that is always included, is surely an abomination to the Lord. And yet millions of Americans, including Christians, waste countless hours in front of their televisions in awe of it.

Among Christians, there is no debating it. There is no excuse for it. You cannot defend such entertainment that portrays excessive violence and profanity and claim to be a true Christian. This would be an oxymoron if ever there was one. Let us consider the following verses that would suggest our evil fantasies could one day become a reality.

> Hear, O earth: behold, I will bring evil
> upon this people, even the fruit of their
> thoughts, because they have not
> hearkened unto my words, nor to my
> law, but rejected it. (Jeremiah 6:19)

We also read of judgments that come in the form of the sins of the people in the Apocrypha. Here, we find specific details regarding strange creatures that people had come to worship. And as a result of their sins, they were plagued with the very creatures that they had idolized.

> In return for their foolish and wicked
> thoughts, which led them astray to
> worship irrational serpents and worth-
> less animals, thou didst send upon them

> a multitude of irrational creatures to punish them, that they might learn that one is punished by the very things by which he sins. Not only could their damage exterminate men, but the mere sight of them could kill by fright.
> (Wisdom of Solomon 11:15, 16, 19)

So as we see, it would not be out of the realm of possibility that we could one day find ourselves in the middle of a real life horror film. If we have succumbed to the idolization of irrational creatures, such as zombies, vampires, etc., then we are in danger of being subjected to such irrational creatures. And when you think of it, the punishment would certainly fit the crime. And millions of people would only be getting what they have been asking for.

Death Is Desired, and Death Is Not Found

During the time of the tribulation, there will be a period when there will be no death, though death will be sought after. There will likely be extreme pain and torment, situations of extreme terror, and yet there will be no escape. When a person has determined to take their own life, it is most often due to a sense of complete hopelessness, and they consider suicide to be their only option. However, during this time frame, there will be no opting out of pain, nor terror. And those who have the mark of the beast will indeed find themselves completely hopeless.

According to the Center for Disease Control and Prevention, the suicide rate in the United States has been rising steadily since the year 2000. With more than 38,000 suicide deaths in 2010, it is among the top 10 leading causes of death in the United States.[3] And among young adults, it is estimated that there are approximately one hundred to two hundred suicide attempts for every completed suicide.

Another disturbing fact concerning the United States is the rise in drug use that we are seeing. According to the Substance Abuse and Mental Health Services Administration, there are more than 22 million Americans that use illicit drugs.[4] As a result of the glamorization of drug use in entertainment, drug abuse has become commonplace in daily life. Also factoring in the state of the economy, many people that face depression will turn to the use of drugs. And the same can be said for the suicide rate as well.

Those who place their faith in man and the government of man are surely facing a hopeless destiny. As the world falls apart, so will everyone that has placed their faith in it. Without Jesus Christ and the evidence of his second coming, we would have no hope whatsoever. Sadly, there are many people that are in this situation. And as times prove to increase with sorrow, many will need to hear the testimony of Jesus Christ.

As the clock races toward the time of the tribulation and a time of trouble such as the world has never seen, we can only expect to witness an unprecedented increase in suicide. As the scriptures foretell, there will be something that prevents death as a means of escape. A disturbing picture of this time is found in a verse from the Apocrypha. And in my opinion, it is directly related to this time frame.

> And there shall be fear and great trembling upon the earth; and those who see that wrath shall be horror stricken, and they shall be seized with trembling." And those who are in the mountains and high lands shall perish of hunger, and they shall eat their own flesh in hunger for bread and drink their own blood in thirst for water.
> (2 Esdras 15:37, 58)

If we are to take this verse literally, it is hard to imagine that people would actually eat their own flesh and drink their own blood. This would be the most desperate attempt to preserve one's life from the threat of starvation. And yet, anyone knows that eating their own flesh and consuming their own blood would ultimately result in the death of their body. That is unless there is knowledge of instances where people have not been dying, even though they have suffered fatal wounds.

This verse could be describing people that are eating the flesh and drinking the blood of their relatives when it uses the key words *their own*. However, considering the verse in Revelation 9, it could very likely be that this verse in the Apocrypha is self- explanatory. One thing that is for sure is that this is one of the most mysterious verses in the book of Revelation.

It is hard to say whether the result of the absence of death is supernatural or some strange phenomenon that can one day be explained through modern science. With all of the horrific chemical and biological uses that are out there today, maybe there will one day be an agent that has an effect that prevents death or prolongs the process of dying.

The time of such horrific circumstances is certainly approaching. Anyone who is not saved and following the Lord will certainly find themselves subject to a chaotic world that is plagued with judgments. The Antichrist will prevail over many but ultimately only over those who receive his mark. As we know, there is a second death. Those who refuse the mark will only be subject to the first. Those who take the mark however will die a second death as well.

The greatest hope that one can have regarding this hellish future is to escape it altogether. Many Christians are confident that they will, in the event of the rapture, which we shall consider in the following chapter.

9

After the Rapture

Among all the prophecies of despair and destruction that are found in the scriptures exists a glimmer of hope—an anticipated event that will allow God's people to escape the great tribulation of the last days. Though you will not find the word rapture in your Bible, it has become the official title word for the event when Christians will be caught up in the clouds. Though the event is viewed the same by most, there are several different doctrines regarding the timing of when it will occur.

The event itself will involve the instantaneous translation of those who are found worthy of escaping not only the rule of the Antichrist but also the wrath of God. It is believed that this could include millions of people all across the world. After the greatest disappearing act that has ever been successfully completed, all those who remain on the earth will be left behind to face the coming horrors of the end times. While the prophecy of this coming event has given many a sense of optimism regarding the last days, it is likely that many who anticipate it will not be included.

When Will It Occur?

As we know, Jesus himself said that no man would know the hour, nor the day. Not even himself or the angels would know, but only the Father. This has been very useful information over the years. It has allowed countless predictions regarding certain dates to be quickly dismissed by true believers. Though we acknowledge that we cannot determine a date for this event, there is still much debate as to what general time frame it will occur.

Like with any prophecy that is found in scripture, the best way to accurately discern the true meaning is to deeply study it. Not only that but to allow the word to truly speak to you, and your ears must be open for the revelation of interpretation. Concerning the prophecy of the rapture, there are three separate views that Christians share regarding the timing of when this event will occur.

Pre-Tribulation Theory

The most popular viewpoint regarding the timing of the rapture is that it will occur prior to the tribulation. In this scenario, the church would be taken out of the world and ascend to heaven before it begins, where they would reside with Jesus for the duration of the seven-year tribulation.

After that seven-year period, the church would return with Christ to rule with him on earth for the one-thousand-year reign.

The pre-tribulation theory is the most widely accepted theory due to there being more scripture to support it than any other. Let us take a look at the scriptures that support a pre-tribulation rapture to determine what they are really saying.

> Then shall two be in the field; the one
> shall be taken, and the other left. Two
> women shall be grinding at the mill; the
> one shall be taken, and the other left.
> Watch therefore: for ye know not what
> hour your Lord doth come. There-fore
> be ye also ready: for in such an hour as
> ye think not the Son of man cometh.
> (Matthew 24:40–42, 44)

In these verses from the book of Matthew, we find very telling information that supports a pre-tribulation scenario. First, Jesus has described to use activities that are business as usual when the rapture occurs. There are two in the field, one is taken and the other is left. There are two women grinding at the mill, one is taken and the other is left. If you have studied the book of Revelation, then you know that the time of the tribulation will be anything but business as usual.

The best evidence from these verses however completely rule out the possibility of a mid to late tribulation rapture. We are given a description of two people working in a field and two women working at a mill. After the Antichrist is given authority to continue for forty-two months, the mark of the beast system is established. Therefore, if this example that Jesus gave us in the book of Matthew were mid to late tribulation, the two in the field and the two at the mill would all have to have the mark of the beast to be employed and working. And as we know, anyone that receives the mark will certainly not be taken to heaven.

> For as a snare shall it come on all them
> that dwell on the face of the whole earth.
> Watch ye therefore, and pray always,
> that ye may be accounted worthy to
> escape all these things that shall come to
> pass, and to stand before the Son of man.
> (Luke 21:35–36)

As we know from studying the book of Revelation, the seven-year period of the tribulation will be plagued with death and destruction. If the rapture were to occur during this time frame, it would certainly come as no surprise. Countless people would be watching for the return of Christ. It would be impossible for the rapture to suddenly come as a snare at such a troubling time period such as the world has never seen.

Also, if Jesus is telling us to pray always, that we would be accounted worthy of escaping all these things, what would we be praying to escape if the tribulation has already begun? These verses seem to speak clearly, and they seem to say that the rapture will occur prior to the tribulation. Let us look at the scripture that is commonly used for the support of a mid and post tribulation rapture.

Mid Tribulation Theory

> And he shall speak great words
> against the most High, and shall wear
> out the saints of the most High, and
> think to change times and laws: and
> they shall be given into his hand until
> a time and times and the dividing of
> time. (Daniel 7:25)

From this verse in the Old Testament concerning the Antichrist, mid tribulation theorists have connected this verse with Revelation 11:11–12. These verses describe the resurrection of the two witnesses. And the assumption has been made that when the voice is heard, saying, "Come up hither," this will be the rapture. However, if we read Revelation 13:5–7, we see a very similar description to Daniel 7:25. When the Antichrist is given power to overcome the saints, it is described as the last half of the tribulation, not the first.

So if the rapture is going to take place at the middle of the tribulation, the best evidence to support it is that the two witnesses hear a voice saying, "Come up hither." But we read no mention of any one else being taken up. And there is no mention of a rapture during this time.

Post Tribulation Theory

> Immediately after the tribulation of those days shall the sun be darkened, and the moon shall not give her light, and the stars shall fall from heaven, and the powers of the heavens shall be shaken: And then shall appear the sign of the Son of man in heaven: and then shall all the tribes of the earth mourn, and they shall see the Son of man coming in the clouds of heaven with power and great glory. And he shall send his angels with a great sound of a trumpet, and they shall gather together his elect from the four winds, from one end of heaven to the other. (Matthew 24:29–31)

These verses from the book of Matthew are one of the key references for the post tribulation rapture theory. However, these verses do not seem to be speaking of the rapture; rather, they are speaking of the second coming. And again, if the rapture were to take place immediately after the tribulation, there would be no need to pray that we are accounted worthy of escaping all these things, as Jesus told us. Another example of key verses for the post tribulation theory is found in the first epistle to the Corinthians. Those who share the post tribulation theory have connected the last trumpet in these verses with the last trumpet in Revelation 11:15.

> Behold, I shew you a mystery; We shall
> not all sleep, but we shall all be changed,
> In a moment, in the twinkling of an eye, at
> the last trump: for the trumpet shall sound,
> and the dead shall be raised incorruptible,
> and we shall be changed.
> (1 Corinthians 15:51–52)

This last trump that Paul is speaking of seems to be mistakenly associated with the seventh trumpet in the book of Revelation. Paul was certainly not giving reference to this, because John did not write the book of Revelation until some forty years later. Also, the seventh trumpet of Revelation is never referred to as "the last trump." It is a trumpet that involves judgment on the earth, not the rapture of the church.

Considering that these verses have been associated due to the word *trumpet*, we would have to recall that there have been many instances of the word *trumpet* in the scriptures. One example would be the feast of trumpets. And the last trumpet, which closes the feast of trumpets is in fact called the last trump. Though this does not necessarily mean that the rapture will occur during the feast of trumpets.

Who Will Be Left?

With a global population of more than seven billion people, there are more than two billion of those who identify themselves as Christians. But does this suggest that two billion people will one day suddenly disappear in the event of the rapture? To find the answer, we must consider what the definition of a Christian is. And just as there are many diverse people in diverse places of the world that make up Christianity, so are there many diverse definitions of what a Christian is.

As we know, the United States of America was founded on Christian principles by our forefathers who were Christian men. This piece of factual history has given much of the world cause to consider us a Christian nation. To appease those who despise Christianity, Barack Obama has publicly stated that we are in fact not a Christian nation. Sadly, while there is some truth to that statement, he spoke of it with a sense of optimism and not disappointment.

As we continue to grow further from the foundational values of our nation, there are those who still identify themselves as Christians simply because of their heritage. Such people that have labeled themselves as Christians simply because of family tradition are not necessarily

Christians at all. If labeling yourself as a Christian is the closest that you get to Christianity, then you are not a Christian. If you are not living your life according to the will of God, then you are not truly following the Lord.

Concerning a loss of foundational values, we must also consider those who identify themselves as liberal Christians. One such church, which claims more than one million members, widely supports gay rights and abortion. Considering that the Bible clearly states that homosexuality is an abomination, it is obvious that such Christians do not regard the word of God. As for the support of the one million abortions each year, which are mostly due to non-medical reasons, they are condoning murder.

We must also consider the multitude of Christians that do not believe in or have sound doctrine regarding the rapture. With more than seven million members, the Jehovah's Witnesses are one such group. As for those who would condone sin and practice sinful acts themselves, the rapture should not even be considered. They should seriously ponder whether or not they will make it to heaven at all.

The Prize of the Overcomer

Considering the multitudes of people that will not be included in the rapture, there will be a large number of those who know the truth. They will find themselves excluded from the rapture as a result of not following the Lord. As the scripture foretells, they will go on to do exploits and to inform those who do not know the truth. Those who are strong in their works and overcome the beast will be well rewarded for their faith.

Let us review the scriptures that speak of this time when Christians will engage in post rapture works and the scriptures that describe the rewards for those who have overcome the tribulation.

> And they that understand among the
> people shall instruct many: yet they
> shall fall by the sword, and by flame,
> by captivity, and by spoil, many days.
> (Daniel 11:33)

In the book of Revelation, after the mark of the beast system has been established, we read that those who die in the Lord thereafter are blessed.

> And I heard a voice from heaven
> saying unto me, write, Blessed are
> the dead which die in the Lord from
> henceforth: Yea, saith the Spirit, that
> they may rest from their labours;
> and their works do follow them.
> (Revelation 14:13)

Considering the viewpoints regarding the timing of the rapture, it would seem that both pre and post tribulation scenarios will unfold. Scripturally speaking, the pre-tribulation rapture is most evident. As for the post tribulation theory, there will in fact be many Christians that will endure the tribulation, not because the rapture hasn't occurred yet but rather because of the fact that they were not accounted worthy of it.

10

Of Death and Damnation

Ever since the time that Adam and Eve resolved to consume the forbidden fruit, death has been a natural part of our lives. An interesting point that my wife has interpreted concerning the truth of God's word is evident in his warning to Adam and Eve. Though the serpent convinced Eve that they would not surely die, they certainly did. And just as God declared that they would die the very day that they ate of the forbidden fruit, they surely did. Because scripture tells us that a day is as a thousand years to the Lord and a thousand years as a day. Considering that man was created for eternal life, the same measure of time would have applied to Adam. All the days of his life were 930 years, so he literally did die the very day that he ate of the fruit.

Though we must all come to terms with our eventual demise, it will only affect our physical bodies. And with the hope that we have in Jesus Christ, we are no longer subject to damnation. When the mark of the beast system is established, the masses will be given a choice of death or damnation. During this time, it is very likely that there will be designated detainment centers for those who oppose the new order.

Detention Centers and Death Camps

Among the many conspiracy theories that surround the new world order is the FEMA camp theory. The premise is that the US government is preparing detention centers for citizens that will pose a threat when the new order is established. Considering that there is scriptural support for such a possibility (Da. 11:33), it is certainly worth considering. Let us first reflect on historical accounts that involved such scenarios.

The most well known example of such tactics would be the Nazi concentration camps of World War II.[1] It is estimated that between 1933 and 1945, there were as many as twenty thousand concentration camps and sub-camps established in Europe. These camps served for the detention of millions of victims that were subjected to forced labor, starvation, and ultimately extermination.

Of the more than 3 million estimated prisoners, these camps not only contained Jews but also political prisoners, people that were determined undesirable due to disabilities, Jehovah's Witnesses, and Catholic clergy members. These prisoners were held without trial or judicial process. While many of the camps were not specifically designed for extermination, many of the prisoners died as a result of starvation, disease, maltreatment, and overwork.[2]

Prisoners that were transported to these camps were often delivered by freight cars. Some of the victims were confined in the boxcars for days and weeks, which resulted in death from dehydration in the summer and freezing to death in the winter. The most infamous method of execution in these camps was the use of gas chambers. Some of these chambers were reportedly capable of containing and killing as many as two thousand victims at a time. The poison gases that were used included carbon monoxide and hydrogen cyanide in the form of Zyklon B.

Many would agree that Hitler himself was a forerunner of the Antichrist. And if the Antichrist will one day reflect similarity to Hitler, we should also expect a reflection of the events that took place during the time of Hitler. And this would certainly include the use of detention centers and death camps. With the planned genocide of the Jewish people, it was obviously a goal of Hitler's to destroy God's people. The Antichrist will desire the same goal, but this time, it will include Christians as well. And this coming evil ruler will be more successful than Hitler, because he will actually conquer the entire world.

As for historical instances of detention camps on US soil, there are numerous examples to consider. Aside from the detention and relocation of the Native Americans[3] when the nation was being formed, there were also detention centers here at home during the Civil War. Located on the Mississippi river, between the cities of Davenport, Iowa, and Rock Island, Illinois, is a 946-acre government site known as Rock Island Arsenal.[4] While it is today the largest government owned weapons manufacturing arsenal, it was once used for a prison camp to house confederate soldiers.

Construction of the prison camp was still underway when the prisoners had begun arriving. In the first month of its use, it is estimated that more than five thousand confederate soldiers were detained there. After the war was over, it is estimated that a total of more than 12,400 confederate soldiers had been detained there.

As well as Germany, the United States also during World War II used detention centers. As a reaction to the bombing of Pearl Harbor in 1941 by Japan, President Roosevelt allowed military commanders to designate regions from which persons may be excluded. This occurred in February of 1942 in accordance with Executive Order 9066.

Under this order, all Japanese and American citizens of Japanese ancestry were to be removed from western coastal regions.[5] It is estimated that there were some 120,000 Japanese citizens and resident Japanese aliens that were relocated to internment camps in numerous states around the country. These camps also housed more than 10,000 Germans, including nearly 5,000 that were transported from Latin American republics.

In 2002, the United States opened an internment camp in Cuba called Guantanamo Bay Detention Camp.[6] Another detention center was opened in Afghanistan called the Bagram Theatre Internment Facility.[7] In accordance with US government policy, many detainees could be held indefinitely without even being legally charged. Another detention center was established in 2003 in Iraq. This center was transformed into an internment and detention camp from a former prison. The name of this center was Abu Ghraib Prison.[8]

So we have historical proof that detention centers have been utilized in the past. Even by the US government. But why is there a growing concern that detention centers will be utilized in the near future? And what evidence is there that would suggest that they will be utilized for us, the American people?

The theory is simply this. As a result of the global economic collapse, which is being orchestrated by those who wish to establish a new world order, many provinces will fall into chaotic darkness. A factual example of this is the Arab spring of 2011. This movement was initiated due to declining economic conditions, and many governments in the Middle East were overthrown by their citizens.

Evidence of such protests have even begun to surface in the US, with the Occupy Wall Street movement. When the meltdown of the economy has taken full effect, it is expected that civil unrest will quickly follow. The disturbing visual of what our country would look like in this scenario does not come from a theory but from factual evidence found in written law. In an event that would allow the president to declare martial law, the constitution would be suspended and the rights of the citizens would be vaporized.

Alarming information regarding a possible suspension of the United States constitution has been publicly discussed for decades. Known as "Garden Plot," and "Rex 84,"[9] which is short for Readiness Exercise 1984, the federal government developed a "scenario and drill" to suspend the constitution and declare martial law. In a possible scenario, military commanders would be placed in charge of state and local governments and would be authorized to detain American citizens who pose a threat to national security.

What is most disturbing about such a scenario is what the government considers to be a threat to national security. Since the time that the Obama regime took over the White House, there have been government lists created which suggest that we the people are in fact the biggest threat to national security.

In a review of these lists, we learn that traditional American citizens who stand for freedom and liberty have been labeled as possible terrorists and are a threat to our way of life here in America. Wait a minute, if those who stand for our traditional way of life are considered a threat to the government, wouldn't that suggest that the government has an anti-American agenda and that they are in fact the biggest threat to our security and way of life? Let us look at the criteria that would label those among us as possible terrorists.

In the 2009 MIAC Strategic Report,[10] the Missouri Information Analysis Center published information regarding the modern militia movement in the United States. In this report, a detailed history of militia activity as well as techniques for identifying militia members was presented to law enforcement agencies such as the Missouri State Highway Patrol. Among the telltale signs of whether or not someone is a militia member and a threat to the government is a list of common indicators.

* *Political Paraphernalia*

Militia members most commonly associate with 3rd party political groups. It is not uncommon for militia members to display Constitutional party, Campaign for Liberty, or Libertarian material. These members are usually supporters of former Presidential Candidates: Ron Paul, Chuck Baldwin, and Bob Barr.

* *Anti-Government Propaganda*

Militia members commonly display pictures, cartoons, bumper stickers that contain anti-government rhetoric. Most of this material will depict the FRS, IRS, FBI, ATF, CIA, UN, Law

Enforcement, and "The New World Order" in a derogatory manner. Additionally, Racial, anti-immigration, and anti-abortion, material may be displayed by militia members.

This report clearly tells us, that we are being labeled as a threat to the government simply by supporting third-party presidential candidates. And if your vehicle displays certain bumper stickers, the law enforcement officer that is driving behind you may consider you as a serious threat. For an example, if you display a bumper sticker that opposes abortion, an officer that is behind you in traffic will automatically remember the stereotyping of government threats that have been published in reports such as this.

Another section of the report includes information regarding the reemergence of the militia movement. It details the conspiracy theories that surround the new world order and suggests that any persons who consider these theories to be real are possible threats to the government as well as all law enforcement agencies.

* Reemergence of the Movement

Newer versions of the NWO conspiracy have been concocted in order to empower the movement. The NWO is seen as using law enforcement, military, national guard, and federal agencies in order to carry out its elitist one world government. Law enforcement and military forces are believed to be utilized in order to confiscate firearms and place individuals into FEMA concentration camps. This scenario has received additional attention due to the US Army NORTHCOM assigning homeland security functions to an active duty Infantry Brigade. The movement sees this brigade as the force that will take their firearms and that the unit is in violation of the Posse Comitatus act.

On a national level, the Department of Homeland Security has labeled Tea party members anti- Fed activists and even veterans returning home from war as potential terrorists. They have also labeled Christians that believe in "end time" prophecy and one world order conspiracies as domestic extremists. Excerpts from the unclassified DHS assessment[11] titled Rightwing Extremism are as follows.

* Economic Hardship and Extremism

> Historically, domestic rightwing extremists have feared, predicted, and anticipated a cataclysmic economic collapse in the United States. Prominent anti-government conspiracy theorists have incorporated aspects of an impending economic collapse to intensify fear and paranoia among like-minded individuals and to attract recruits during times of economic uncertainty. Conspiracy theories involving declarations of martial law, impending civil strife or racial conflict, suspension

of the U.S. Constitution, and the creation of citizen detention camps often incorporate aspects of a failed economy. Anti-government conspiracy theories and "end times" prophecies could motivate extremist individuals and groups to stockpile food, ammunition, and weapons. These teachings also have been linked with the radicalization of domestic extremist individuals and groups in the past, such as violent Christian Identity organizations and extremist members of the militia movement.

* Legislative and Judicial Drivers

Many right-wing extremist groups perceive recent gun control legislation as a threat to their right to bear arms and in response have increased weapons and ammunition stockpiling, as well as renewed participation in paramilitary training exercises. Such activity, combined with a heightened level of extremist paranoia, has the potential to facilitate criminal activity and violence. During the 1990s, rightwing extremist hostility toward government was fueled by the implementation of restrictive gun laws—such as the Brady Law that established a 5-day waiting period prior to purchasing a handgun and the 1994 Violent Crime Control and Law Enforcement Act that limited the sale of various types of assault rifles—and federal law enforcement's handling of the confrontations at Waco, Texas and Ruby Ridge, Idaho.

*   Disgruntled Military Veterans

DHS/I&A assesses that rightwing extremists will attempt to recruit and radicalize returning veterans in order to exploit their skills and knowledge derived from military training and combat. These skills and knowledge have the potential to boost the capabilities of extremists—including lone wolves or small terrorist cells—to carry out violence. The willingness of a small percentage of military personnel to join extremist groups during the 1990s because they were disgruntled, disillusioned, or suffering from the psychological effects of war is being replicated today.

*   Lone Wolves and Small Terrorist Cells

DHS/I&A assesses that lone wolves and small terrorist cells embracing violent rightwing extremist ideology are the most dangerous domestic terrorism threat in the United States. Information from law enforcement and nongovernmental organizations indicates lone wolves and small terrorist cells have shown intent—and, in some cases, the capability—to commit violent acts.

Was it just me, or was the entire country under the impression that Homeland Security was established to protect us from the Islamic extremist threat from foreign countries? These reports and assessments seem to only suggest that there was a dark agenda behind the raised security measures that resulted from the events of 9/11. So we see that the American people are suspect to the government, but what measures would be taken in the event that martial law is declared? As you will see, the following Executive orders[12] will completely strip us of our rights, and our freedoms.

> * Executive order 10990 allows the government to take over all modes of transportation and control of highways and seaports.
> * Executive order 10995 allows the government to seize and control the communication media.
> * Executive order 10997 allows the government to take over all electrical power, gas, petroleum, fuels, and minerals.
> * Executive order 11000 allows the government to mobilize US civilians into work brigades under government supervision.
> * Executive order 11003 allows the government to take over all airports and aircraft, including commercial aircraft.
> * Executive order 11004 allows the housing and finance authority to relocate and establish new locations for the population.

These are just a few examples of the many Executive Orders that could be utilized in the event that the president would declare martial law. But we shouldn't worry about such grim scenarios, lest we be labeled paranoid extremists by the government that established such laws. We see that the government views Christians that believe in end-time prophecy, which is the word of God, and that oppose abortion, which is the murder of innocent babies, to be radical extremists.

This paints a clear picture of how we will be considered a threat in the last days. Those who oppose the mark of the beast system will be labeled as radical extremists, who are comparing current world events with end-time prophecy. There is no doubt that there will be detention centers for such dissidents; the word of God in the book of Revelation tells us that there will be martyrs that are beheaded.

Though America was founded by Christian men and is predominantly Christian today, it will fall under the same tyranny as the rest of the world. It will be no exception when the Antichrist comes to power. And who knows, he may begin his reign from the White House. If he does, all the measures are being taken to help the government identify you as an extreme threat to national security. Today terror suspects are checked for bombs; tomorrow, they will be checked for Bibles.

The Point of No Return

As we live under the grace of God, we are afforded reconciliation and forgiveness when we stumble during our walk of faith. However, anyone who receives the mark of the beast will not be granted forgiveness. According to the scriptures, there is only one sin that cannot be forgiven. That sin is blasphemy against the Holy Spirit.

> Wherefore I say unto you, All manner of sin and blasphemy shall be forgiven unto men: but the blasphemy against the Holy Ghost shall not be forgiven unto men. And whosoever speaketh a word against the Son of man, it shall be forgiven him: but whosoever speaketh against the Holy Ghost, it shall not be forgiven him, neither in this world, neither in the world to come. (Matthew 12:31–32)

Considering that this sin is the only one that is unforgivable, as Jesus himself stated, there must be a connection between it and the mark of the beast. As we read from the book of Revelation, those who receive the mark of the beast will suffer both in this world and the world to come.

> And the third angel followed them,
> saying with a loud voice, If any man
> worship the beast and his image, and
> receive his mark in his forehead, or in
> his hand, The same shall drink of the
> wine of the wrath of God, which is
> poured out without mixture into the
> cup of his indignation; and he shall be
> tormented with fire and brimstone in
> the presence of the holy angels, and in
> the presence of the Lamb: And the
> smoke of their torment ascendeth up
> for ever and ever: and they have no
> rest day nor night, who worship the
> beast and his image, and whosoever
> receiveth the mark of his name.
> (Revelation 14:9–11)

Another verse connecting the sin of blasphemy with the mark of the beast is also found in the book of Revelation. In John's vision of the beast kingdom, he sees the name of *blasphemy* written upon their heads.

> And I stood upon the sand of the sea,
> and saw a beast rise up out of the sea,
> having seven heads and ten horns,
> and upon his horns ten crowns, and
> upon his heads the name of
> blasphemy. (Revelation 13:1)

When the mark of the beast is made manifest, it will be obvious to us that know the truth. It would not be the nature of God to condemn a person for partaking in something that they did not know was a sin. It will likely incorporate blasphemy, which would be an obvious sign that it is an unforgivable sin. During the time of the tribulation, desperate measures will drive many to accept the mark. Both those who know the truth and those who have not regarded it will willingly take the mark of the beast.

Life Goes On, but Not for Long

For those who commit spiritual suicide by accepting the mark, their life will only continue for a short period. However, under stressful and chaotic circumstances, a short time can seem like an eternity. In the book of Revelation, the mark of the beast system is described as being enforced after the middle of the seven-year tribulation. This would only leave three and a half years to live for those who accept the mark. Let us consider in detail exactly what life will be like for those three and a half years.

Supernatural Disasters

When Jesus was asked what the signs of the end would be, earthquakes were one of the signs that he described. As we have seen in the last decade alone, there has been an intensified amount of earthquakes around the globe.

These earthquakes have been powerful, causing tsunami waves and claiming the lives of nearly one million people. These earthquakes however have been the result of natural occurrences. During the tribulation, there will be earthquakes that are specifically caused by supernatural judgments. These earthquakes will likely be off the scale and will instill terror in the hearts of all the inhabitants of the earth.

Other supernatural disasters include the loss of all water on earth. The sea becomes as the blood of a dead man, and the rivers and the fountains become blood. Men will be scorched with extreme heat as a result of a judgment that involves the sun. This judgment of heat occurs after the waters have been turned to blood.

Intense Pain and Torment

Among the judgments will be supernatural occurrences that cause intense pain and suffering. From the description in the book of Revelation, it is obvious that there will be no medications that offer relief from the pain. There will be no escaping it and no option but to suffer through it.

> And the fifth angel poured out his vial upon the seat of the beast; and his kingdom was full of darkness; and they gnawed their tongues for pain, And blasphemed the God of

heaven because of their pains and
their sores, and repented not of their
deeds. (Revelation 16:10–11)

Increase in Wickedness

Considering that the entire world will be under the rule of an evil dictatorship, wickedness will increase through laws and policies. We should also consider that at this point the rapture has occurred, taking away the most compassionate people that society depends on in troubling times. Without the help of the church, there will be nowhere to turn in such chaotic, disastrous times.

We have read that there will be Christians who know the truth during the tribulation that will help and inform others. However, according to the following verses, they will be few and far between.

> Behold, the days come, saith the Lord God,
> that I will send a famine in the land, not a
> famine of bread, nor a thirst for water, but
> of hearing the words of the Lord: And they
> shall wander from sea to sea, and from the
> north even to the east, they shall run to and
> fro to seek the word of the Lord, and shall
> Not find it. (Amos 8:11–12)

11

Hell Lies Waiting

The only thing that remains for those who accept the mark of the beast is judgment and damnation. This will result in the eternal separation from the presence of God. If this were not bad enough, those who accept the mark will share eternity with Satan and the fallen angels, the Antichrist, demons, murderers, and all the evil spirits that have lived in the earth since the beginning of time.

Today, there are millions of Christians that do not believe in the literal existence of hell. Denominations such as the Jehovah's Witnesses and Seventh Day Adventists believe in a doctrine called soul sleep. They teach that hell is no more than the common grave, and that when you die, you become nonexistent. The basis for this doctrine comes from only two instances in scripture. One is that "the dead know nothing" (Ec. 9:5), and two, Jesus said that Lazarus was sleeping when he was actually dead (John 11:11).

Let us consider the reality of hell as it is described in the

Bible. According to Strong's exhaustive concordance of the

Bible, there are fifty-three instances of the word hell in the scriptures, which provide more than enough evidence to prove that hell is a literal place of punishment.

The Atmosphere of Hell

According to scripture, the location of hell is in the depths of the earth. It is always described as being down and more specifically is referred to as being in the nether parts of the earth (Ez. 31:18) and very deep (Job 11:8). Scholars believe that it was created just prior to or during the six days of creation. It was not created for mankind, and men were not intended to inhabit it. However, because of the fall of Adam, the gates of hell were opened to us all. In the following verse, Jesus describes who this place was originally created for.

> Then shall He say also unto them on the left hand, Depart from me, ye cursed, into everlasting fire, prepared for the devil and his angels. (Matthew 25:41)

This verse tells us that hell was originally intended for Satan and the fallen angels. It also tells us that they will not be the only beings that inhabit it. The following verses give us a detailed description of a man in hell. They not only indicate that this is a real place of torment but also that we will have all five senses that our physical flesh bodies have and that we will not simply be ghostly figures.

> And in hell he lift up his eyes, being in
> torments, and seeth Abraham afar off,
> and Lazarus in his bosom. And he cried
> and said, Father Abraham, have mercy on
> me, and send Lazarus, that he may dip
> the tip of his finger in water, and cool my
> tongue; for I am tormented in this flame.
> (Luke 16:23–24)

The Jewish historian Josephus, who lived ad 37 to ad 100, also described the atmosphere of the underworld and Abraham's bosom. The following is an extract from Josephus's discourse to the Greeks concerning hades.[1]

> 1. Now as to Hades, wherein the souls of the righteous and unrighteous are detained, it is necessary to speak of it. Hades is a place in the world not regularly finished; a subterraneous region, wherein the light of this world does not shine; from which circumstance, that in this region the light does not shine, it cannot be but there must be in it perpetual darkness. This region is allotted as a place of custody for souls, in which angels are appointed as guardians to them, who distribute to them temporary punishments, agreeable to every one's behavior and manners.
>
> 2. In this region there is a certain place set apart, as a lake of unquenchable fire, where into we suppose no one hath hitherto been cast; but it is prepared

for a day afore-determined by God, in which one righteous sentence shall deservedly be passed upon all men; when the unjust, and those that have been disobedient to God, and have given honor to such idols as have been the vain operations of the hands of men, as to God himself, shall be adjudged to this everlasting punishment, as having been the causes of defilement; while the just shall obtain an incorruptible and never-fading kingdom. These are now indeed confined in Hades, but not in the same place wherein the unjust are confined.

3. For there is one descent into this region, at whose gate we believe there stands an archangel with an host; which gate when those pass through that are conducted down by the angels appointed over souls, they do not go the same way; but the just are guided to the right hand, and are led with hymns, sung by the angels appointed over that place, unto a region of light, in which the just have dwelt from the beginning of the world; not constrained by necessity, but ever enjoying the prospect of the good things they see, and rejoice in the expectation of those new enjoyments which will be peculiar to every one of them, and esteeming those things beyond what we have here; with whom there is no place of toil, no burning heat, no piercing cold, nor are any briers there; but the countenance of the fathers and of the

just, which they see always smiles upon them, while they wait for that rest and eternal new life in heaven, which is to succeed this region. This place we call The Bosom of Abraham.

4. But as to the unjust, they are dragged by force to the left hand by the angels allotted for punishment, no longer going with a good-will, but as prisoners driven by violence; to whom are sent the angels appointed over them to reproach them and threaten them with their terrible looks, and to thrust them still downwards. Now those angels that are set over these souls drag them into the neighborhood of hell itself; who, when they are hard by it, continually hear the noise of it, and do not stand clear of the hot vapor itself; but when they have a near view of this spectacle, as of a terrible and exceeding great prospect of fire, they are struck with a fearful expectation of a future judgment, and in effect punished thereby: and not only so, but where they see the place [or choir] of the fathers and of the just, even hereby are they punished; for a chaos deep and large is fixed between them; insomuch that a just man that hath compassion upon them cannot be admitted, nor can one that is unjust, if he were bold enough to attempt it, pass over it.

From the book of Enoch,[2] concerning his vision of the underworld, we find another telling description of hell. Again, we have the description of a burning place of torment that was originally intended for Satan and the fallen angels.

> 5. And from thence I went to another place, which was still more horrible than the former, and I saw a horrible thing: a great fire there which burnt and blazed, and the place was cleft as far as the abyss, being full of great descending columns of fire: neither its extent or magnitude could I see, nor could I conjecture.
>
> 6. Then I said: How fearful is the place and how terrible to look upon!
>
> 7. Then Uriel answered me, one of the holy angels who was with me, and said unto me: Enoch, why hast thou such fear and affright? And I answered: Because of this fearful place, and because of the spectacle of the pain.
>
> 8. And he said unto me: This place is the prison of the angels, and here they will be imprisoned for ever.

From the Bible, we have more than enough information to convince us that hell is a literal place. Let us look at a few verses that detail the nature of it and what the effects of inhabiting it will be.

Hell is eternal, burning with fire.

And the smoke of their torment ascendeth up for ever and ever; And they have no rest day or night. (Revelation 14:11)
And the devil that deceived them was cast into the lake of fire and brimstone, where the beast and the false prophet are, and shall be tormented day and night for ever and ever.

(Revelation 20:10)

Hell is a place of conscious torment.

Furnace of fire...weeping and gnashing of teeth. (Mathew 13:50)
Where their worm dieth not, and the fire is not Quenched. (Mark 9:48)
He will be tormented with fire and brimstone.

(Revelation 14:10)

The descriptions of hell from the Bible prove to us that hell is very real. And those who go to dwell there will find themselves in a state of pain that can be felt by a living flesh body. If those who are righteous will have glorified bodies in the afterlife, it only makes sense that the unrighteous will have bodies also, though they will not be glorified. The following list makes this very clear to us.

Five Senses Used in Hell

* Touch: pain from burning fire
* Taste: extreme thirst, dry mouth
* Sight: fire, smoke, darkness
* Smell: rotting garbage-gehenna, brimstone
* Sound: weeping, crying, moaning, screaming

Subterranean Cities

During the time of the tribulation, John has written that there will be many people that attempt to hide underground—from the plagues, natural disasters, chaos, and ultimately from the wrath of God. Let us look at the verse and discern all the different types of men that will hide beneath the earth.

> And the kings of the earth, and the great men, and the rich men, and the chief captains, and the mighty men, and every bondman, and every free man, hid themselves in the dens and in the rocks of the mountains.
> (Revelation 6:15)

When we think of underground living quarters, most of us envision small, closed in bunkers, such as the likes of those that preppers and survivalists construct for a worst case scenario. However, as bizarre as it may sound, there are hundreds of large cities under the earth across the entire world. In the United States alone, there are dozens of underground cities that most of us never knew existed.

In Albany, New York, beneath the Empire State Plaza,[3] lies an underground city that has banks, restaurants, a YMCA, and even a police station. Beneath the city of Chicago lies a tunnel system spanning more than forty city blocks and is known as the Chicago Pedway.[4] My wife personally heard the testimony of a truck driver that had just come home from delivering her first shipment into an underground city. She was shocked to learn first hand that there were businesses and even living space beneath the city of Chicago.

Aside from the dozens of underground cities that can be inhabited by the public, the secretive, well-guarded government underground cities are suspected to number in the hundreds. Most of these underground networks are mysteriously within close proximity to railroad tracks and airports. One such underground city that has drawn extensive attention from conspiracy theorists is actually located directly beneath an airport.

The Denver International Airport[5] is located twenty-five miles from Denver and sits on more than thirty-three thousand acres in the middle of nowhere. It has it's own solar farm, which sits on more than seven acres, and uses 9,200 solar panels, which produce over three million kilowatt hours of energy each year. With more than thirty-three thousand acres of land, Denver International is without contest the largest land area airport in the United States. The second largest, which pales in comparison, is Dallas/Fort Worth with eighteen thousand acres.

Though you won't find access to the underground through the airport, there are more than enough photos and eye witness accounts of extensive excavation and underground construction. The strangest aspect of this airport however is the artwork that is found inside. There are large murals that depict dying children and animals. There is a large soldier holding a machine gun in one hand and a sword in the other. The sword is painted in a swooping motion above a dove as though it is about to kill it. As we know, the dove is a symbol of peace and Christianity. There is also a stone on display with the symbol of freemasonry. Below the date on the stone are the mysterious words "New World Airport Commission."

The theory concerning this airport is the same theory regarding all secretive underground locations. When the world falls apart, the elite will go underground. And in this case, it will be conveniently located beneath a large airport. All they would have to do in the event of a major crisis is hop a flight to Denver and not even worry about having to leave the airport.

Over the past few decades, much information has come out regarding deep underground government installations.

Whistle blowers have informed the public through lectures, articles, and many books that have been published. One such whistle blower was a government geologist named Phil Schneider.[6] He was in the process of debriefing the public at town hall meetings and through a book he was working on when he was found dead in 1996.

Having began his work as a geologist for black ops secret underground bases in the 1970s, his initial assumption was that these bases were for national security measures. After learning that there was a dark, sinister agenda behind these installations, he left his work in a patriotic attempt to inform the public of all that he knew. His main point that he discussed was that there is a new world order agenda and plans to establish it by no later than the year 2025.

These underground cities, as he described them, were as deep as a mile beneath the surface and interconnected by a maglev rail system. At the time of his last lecture in 1995, he estimated that there were as many as 130 of these underground installations across the country. He stated that the cost of each one of these installations was around 17 billion dollars and that the annual black ops budget was in the neighborhood of a half trillion dollars a year at that time.

He stated that the black budget is not monitored by congress and that it is an independent taxing body that is mainly funded by drug operations by the CIA, NSA, and the Drug Enforcement Administration. The new world order as he described it is a plan to bring the entire world under one authority, after the masses have been disarmed, and bankrupted. He stated that there is a sinister force behind the new world order agenda, and that it is not just the work of man.

This force, he claimed, is a race of alien entities, that co-habit these subterranean installations with humans. Obviously, he loses credibility when it comes to the E.T agenda. Many people undoubtedly write off everything that he has disclosed concerning these underground bases. However, if you know your Bible as I do, then you would not write him off as easily as most.

First of all, we know that the last world empire will be under the control of Satan and that there will be an evil world wide ruling party. To assume that mankind will establish this empire without the help of demonic forces would be incorrect. Ezekiel described a strange chariot that was in the sky. If we saw this today, it would be called a UFO. In the epistle of Jude, we read references to fallen angels and a description of "wandering stars." Have you ever seen the unexplainable eyewitness videos of those lights that swarm around in the sky? They look like wandering stars.

There has been too much disclosure from former employees of NASA, government officials, military officers, etc. regarding a cover up of unknown life-forms and alien technology for us to ignore. I do not believe that there are aliens from other planets, but I know that there are demons. There has been an agenda for more than seventy years now to convince us that there are beings from other planets. Why?

When the truth comes out, the public will be more accepting of "friends from outer space" than they will be of demonic beings bent on destruction. To my surprise, the Pope even commented recently on the possibility of alien beings visiting earth in the future.[7] Seriously, is he that ill informed? What next, is the Vatican going to launch a mission to Mars?

One thing is for sure, there is certainly something going on beneath the earths surface. Along with all the eyewitness accounts of these underground installations, there has also been a dramatic increase in earthquakes in the past few years. There have also been reports in the Midwest of unusual rumbling and roaring noises[8] when there haven't even been earthquakes. While all of these occurrences and conspiracy theories are very strange, it all makes good sense when you read the Bible.

Darkness and Eternal Torment

For those who are subject to spend eternity in hell, the worst part is not the horrific beings that they will share it with, but the eternal separation from the presence of God. Imagine the worst day that you have ever had, and yet the presence of God was all around you. Imagine if there was no light on earth or birds or any good thing whatsoever. Imagine the world without Godly people that are always willing to help and pray for you. This is what eternity will look like for those who are slaves to their sins.

You may ask where the proof of an existing hell can be found or what will be our warning sign to avoid it. Both the proof and the warning are found in the scriptures. There is no need for scientific proof or further warning if it is the word of God. Let us look at the verse that clearly tells us that we need look no further than the scriptures to find proof of this place of punishment.

> For I have five brethren; that he may
> testify unto them, lest they also come
> into this place of torment. Abraham
> saith unto him, They have Moses and
> the prophets; let them hear them.
> (Luke 16:28–29)

12

When Our Leaders Become Lawless

"When the righteous are in authority, the people rejoice: but when the wicked beareth rule, the people mourn" (Proverbs 29:2) . In our nation as of late, would you say that the church has been mournful? We have witnessed the wicked rejoicing over state laws allowing them to marry their own sex and the legalization of marijuana. But the wise are surely mournful. For they know that judgment will surely befall the nation regarding its ungodly laws. Let us consider the changes that are swiftly dividing our land.

Leaders in the Church

It's happening all over the world. But not like here at home. Pastors, mega churches, and entire church denominations are denying the Word of God to appease the masses, to accept gay marriage, and to ultimately lie to the gay community by leading them to believe that God accepts their lifestyle. This would be the equivalent of Lot announcing that God accepted this lifestyle to the people of Sodom, just before God destroyed it with fire. While I have no diploma in theology as of yet, nor claim to be a Bible scholar, it is simply a no-brainer that this movement we are witnessing is not of God.

Undoubtedly, there are those who claim such views as mine to be from the Old Testament and irrelevant today. However, I must remind them that we serve a God that does not change, also that the same decrees are found in the New Testament:

> Know ye not that the unrighteous shall not inherit the kingdom of God? Be not deceived: neither fornicators, nor idolaters, nor adulterers, nor effeminate, nor abusers of themselves with mankind, Nor thieves, nor covetous, nor drunkards, nor revilers, nor extortioners, shall inherit the kingdom of God. (1 Corinthians 6:9–10)

Be not deceived! Ministers have been deceived and are deceiving many as we speak. Why do we not hear of large congregations walking out of the church when such deception comes from the mouth of a pastor? They are being deceived. This is a major red flag, people. There has been debate for much time over such things as the consumption of alcohol, the use of tobacco, dress code, and on and on among Christians. But this is another level. No, this must be another planet. It shouldn't be up for debate. It is indeed a sign of the time—the major increase of godlessness, lawlessness, and all things abominable that usher in the worldwide theater of the apocalypse. Were we not called to be the salt of the earth? And now the ministers pour forth sugar to sweeten the sinner?

It's an old truth that withstands the test of time. *The truth hurts.* If you love people as commanded by the gospel, you would inform the sinner of the sin that stands between themselves and God. You should not lie to them, unless you hate them and yourself. Does Jesus accept such sinners? Of course He does! But not their baggage of sin. We must all repent, seek forgiveness. Get as far away from that sin as possible! And for those sitting in the pews, get as far away from that liar as possible! If he or she is teaching deception, you better call them on it!

Leaders of the Nation

As the wicked demand to be justified, the lawmakers give in. The righteous are thrown under the bus. We need to be more vocal on the issues that are going to destroy our foundation. I encouraged everyone to voice their opinion to the United States Supreme Court as they were considering the debate as to whether or not same sex marriage would become legal nationwide. Unfortunately our lawless leaders passed the abomination of a law. And sadly the Christian voice was not heard in their decision, yet we must not get so discouraged that we cease to make our voices heard. Below is a copy of the text which I personally submitted.

> Supreme Court of the United States
> 1 First Street, NE
> Washington, DC 20543
> April 28, 2015
>
> Dear Supreme Court Justices,
>
> I would first like to thank you for your time and service to our great country. I realize that you have very important decisions to make regarding sensitive issues this year. The debate which demands my opinion to be voiced, is one that deeply concerns Christians in America. It is an evil agenda born of the depraved, under the guise of freedom. Who's goals are to undermine God, His covenants and His people. The advocates for same sex marriage demand to have something that is not theirs. They disregard the fact that it is forbidden them. And they now demand that lawmakers justify their opposition to God. History is not hidden from us. Many have perished in ancient times for our ensample. As you well know, sodomy is the foundation on which same sex marriages are based. The word sodomy is derived from the ancient city of Sodom, Which was destroyed by fire for the forbidden sexual practices of it's people.

I ask that you please consider the fact that the world is watching. Your decision on this matter could strongly effect decisions around the world. More importantly than this, God is watching. And He decrees judgments according to our actions. To make lawful the things which God has determined unlawful, is to openly mock God. But we know the Holy Scriptures concerning this. "Be not deceived: God is not mocked: for whatsoever a man soweth, that shall he also reap." Galatians 6:7. I request that you make no hesitation to strike down the demands of the wicked. Who's desires are the corruption of our country, and the demoralization of it's citizens. In no way do I request this on my own behalf. For it's personal effects on myself are not evident. But on the behalf of a great nation, that was founded by Christian leaders, who acknowledged the principals of God.

Our common goals for a prosperous future are at stake. My wife and I have, however been shown dreams and visions of a dark and terrible fate. Riots, fires, famine, earthquakes and ultimately an enemy invasion in the midst of this instability. Such destruction eventually plagues those who defiantly oppose God. We have prayed. We will continue to pray. The future that we have seen must be changed. Only know this, if it is not changed, God will defend those who judged wisely. But a bitter end awaits those who did not. "If He condemned the cities of Sodom and Gomorrah by burning them to ashes, and made

them an example of what is going to happen to the ungodly; and if He rescued Lot, a righteous man, who was distressed by the depraved conduct of the lawless (for that righteous man, living among them day after day, was tormented in his righteous soul by the lawless deeds he saw and heard.) If this is so, then the Lord knows how to rescue the godly from trials and to hold the unrighteous for punishment on the day of judgment." 2 Peter 2:6–9
Yours sincerely,

Woodrow Polston

We must be diligent. We have given up too much already. Consider the dark future that awaits our children. The world is running out of safe havens for Christians. The persecution has begun. Tribulation is evident. Our King is coming soon. And let our works stand as a witness against the wicked, who would not heed the warning signs.

The Vision of Judgment

There have been many men of God that have shared dreams and visions of a coming dark fate for America. Some of them recorded decades apart. Having had recurring dreams myself of our skies being filled with foreign fighter jets and my wife's recurring dreams of earthquakes and a possible foreign occupation, we have researched the possibility and reached certain conclusions. Please keep in mind that all things must fall into place for such a scenario to unfold.

Since we began to question the possibility of this event several years ago, many signs have come to pass that would suggest that things are certainly falling into place. Two of those major signs are as follows: our deteriorating relations with Russia due to imposing sanctions against them and, as equally important, our waning friendship with Israel. Having put aside all the abominable sins that would prompt swift judgment on America, there is one future action that will cause all these terrors to instantly befall us. That action would be our involvement in the persuasion of Israel to divide Jerusalem.

When Jerusalem is divided as it is written in Revelation, if we have any role in it, our nation will be divided likewise. Without discussing a long list of those who have seen this coming, or all of the details included, this is a summary of the prophetic vision as it has been seen. There will be a major earthquake on the New Madrid fault line. It will divide the United States without notice. The instant disruption of travel and commerce will plunge the country into chaos, which will involve major crime waves in the form of looting, rioting, home invasions, and all such robberies and rampant murder. In the midst of this chaos, we will be invaded by Russian forces.

Having considered this vision as a real possibility, there have been many questions concerning what we as

Americans should do in such an event. If you imagine the scenario, you likely bring the classic film *Red Dawn* to mind and easily visualize yourself among a group of well-armed patriots defending our land. However, if like myself you seek to do accordingly to the will of God, you may consider a more peaceful approach. If our nation is judged in this manner, it will certainly be the will of God. If we fight it, would we not be fighting the will of God?

Consider this excerpt from Jeremiah when Israel was invaded by its enemies as a judgment from God:

> I spoke also to Zed-e-kiah king of Judah according to all these words, saying, Bring your necks under the yoke of the king of Babylon, and serve him and his people, and live. Why will ye die, thou and thy people, by the sword, by the famine, and by the pestilence, as the Lord hath spoken against the nation that will not serve the king of Babylon? (Jeremiah 27:12–13)

If like myself, you have taken notice of the mounting ungodliness in our nation, such a judgment would come as little surprise. However there are growing multitudes of Christians in this nation that have saturated themselves in the things of the world, to such an extent that they are literally clueless as to what is really going on around them. Such an event will suddenly grip them by surprise, much like the terror attacks on 9/11. Only this time it will be crippling. And we will not be able to continue on in arrogance and defiance of God. Life will go on, but America will not resemble her former glory. There will be a way made for God's people here. Only they will stand and prosper in an otherwise devastating state. They will eat and feed others. They will rise and do the works of God in a land that has become estranged to God.

In the dreams and visions that my wife and I have received from God, there is both comfort and despair. The events that will be taking place are very troubling. However God will both protect and provide for His people. My wife has seen both a church and a large property that we will establish for an end-time harvest. She lay out the design for the church on our computer in a few short hours. I was amazed. It was far beyond anything you would expect in such little time. Concerning the property, it was a thousand-acre farm, which will thrive in a time of drought and famine. I believe that there are many of God's people who are receiving instruction for divine purpose right now through dreams and visions. And there will be many more who will very soon.

13

Righteousness Prevails

Though the world will only become more evil and senseless as we approach the end, the outcome will be a victorious overthrow by the King that is destined to reign. As we grow ever closer to his return, we are witnessing a worldwide brutal campaign against his people. Aside from the more than 150,000 estimated believers that are martyred each year for their faith abroad, there is a systematic agenda that has been unfolding here in the United States for some time.

This agenda has successfully changed the morality of our society. Through the outlets of entertainment, availability of narcotics, and establishment of ungodly laws, our nation has been transformed into what it is today—a cesspool of bankrupted, divorced, drug addicted, alcoholic, selfish heathens that do not know how to live. The answer as to whether or not our country has a chance, lies in the hands of the people. Will they wake up and realize that Jesus is the solution and that they need to seek him?

At this point of time in our nation's history, it should be clear to everyone that there is no solution to our problems that can be offered by man or man's government. Morals and values aside, the economic state of our nation could only leave the simple minded with any optimism. And as we know, they will be lining up as far as the eye can see to elect the liar we know as the Antichrist.

The War on Christianity

From the time that the war was officially waged on family values and more specifically on Christian family values, the results have been catastrophic. When prayer was removed from public schools in 1962, the biggest concerns regarding students were dress code violation, chewing gum in class, and running in the halls. Today, the concerns are murder, drug addiction, rape, alcohol abuse, and teen pregnancy.

As a result of numerous deadly shooting incidents that have occurred in public schools, many citizens have sought a solution to prevent these senseless acts. Some feel that tighter gun control will be the answer, and communist regimes such as China have even stated that American citizens should be disarmed.[1] Yeah, is that not a sign that we should keep our arms or what? Such citizens that seek gun confiscation as a result of school shootings are the very people that vote for the murder of one million unborn babies in this nation every year.

This is somewhat hypocritical, is it not? If they condone the slaughter known as abortion, why do they pretend to be so upset when children are victims of a school shooting? I will tell you why. Because they want our guns. They do not care about these children, and they use such a crisis as an opportunity to take away the rights of those who do care and prove that they care by voting against such senseless acts as abortion.

Creating an unstable environment at school was not enough, so the home life of average American citizens was also a key target. The successful strategies that would create broken homes across the nation were hidden behind movements such as women's liberation.[2] Funded by the Rockefeller Foundation, a member of the family explained that it was a no-brainer. With women joining the workforce across the nation, not only would the taxable population double, but children without a permanent homebody would depend more on the government-run schools. Additionally, the children would learn their moral values from television, which is also under the control of the elite banking cartels.

Through the outlets of the media, which include television, film, commercials, music, and magazines, a campaign of brainwashing has destroyed the moral values of our society. In popular women's magazines, women are urged to have sex on the first date and given tips for being promiscuous. There is no mention of family or children. Gay rights are pushed through these outlets and basically everything that contradicts the way that we should live according to the word of God.

In 1962, the debate was whether or not removing prayer from school was a positive decision for our nation. Today, there is debate as to whether or not gay marriage is a positive decision. Who with a mind of their own could see any of these topics as being rational? Could women's liberation and feminist movements also be responsible for an increase in homosexuality? If the role of the woman in society has been dramatically changed, this could explain why some men have sexually disassociated themselves with women. Let us take a look at some of the statistics that show us the results of the agenda to demoralize our society.

* *Pre-television, women's liberation, prayer ban*

1940–1950 divorce rate–2.5% of population [3]
1940–1950 marriage rate–12.4% of population [4]
1940–1950 non-marital birth rate–3.8% of population [5]

* *Post-television, women's liberation, prayer ban*

Present-day divorce rate–4.0% of population [6]
Present-day marriage rate–7.1% of population [7]
Present-day non-marital birth rate–33.0% of population [8]

As we can see from just a few common statistics, the American family household has been seriously assaulted. It would seem as though there is no time to spare for reading the Bible. The time allotment has been replaced by media that encourages adultery, divorce, drug abuse, and violence. Because the American people are subjecting themselves to this brainwashing, our nation is in a perilous state.

The current state of American society being what it is really makes me wonder how the majority of our citizens identify themselves as Christians. If we practically make up the nation, then why do so many voters elect politicians that pass ungodly laws during elections? Do these people simply label themselves as Christians because they consider themselves closer to a Christian than a worshipper of some strange cow god or something? Or are they really Christians that are that far out of touch with the reality of God's word?

As legalized marijuana and gay marriage are becoming a reality, they will soon be commonplace, just as abortion has been commonplace for more than forty years now. It is also very likely that there will be a successful gun grab in the near future. As we know, the original purpose of the Second Amendment was to keep an equal balance between the citizens and the government. What many do not realize is that this balance has not existed for many years now. Citizens are not allowed to own fully automatic weapons, explosives, or any number of advanced weapons that the government has.

Many fear that there will be a ban on all semi-automatic weapons, and we will be left with only old relics of the past.

In reality, that is the case already when you consider your options of firearms verses what the government has. The buzz about disarming the American people usually leads to the discussion of a possible civil war. However, such a war would be futile. We would have UN troops, NATO troops, and God only knows how many foreign soldiers rampaging through our nation. And that would be in addition to all the US troops and alphabet agencies such as the DHS, BATFE, FBI, NSA, etc.

As we have seen from examples such as the MIAC report and DHS Assessment report, there is already a campaign to make conservative gun owners a target. Even displaying Christian values, such as anti-abortion bumper stickers, is considered seditious paraphernalia. Let's face it, if you believe your Bible as I do, our world is going to be in a horrible state before it's all said and done. We should not be shocked when ungodly laws are passed. Rather, we should be expecting them to come into legislation and be ready to protest them and vote them out. If we had been more proactive in the past, maybe things would not be so out of control today. Let us take a look at the liberal logic that has supported the agenda of destroying our nation.

* *Goal: Ban prayer from school, teach evolution*

Outcome: High teen pregnancy rate, high birth rate of unwanted children

* *Solution: Abortion*

Establish law to murder unwanted children, teach sexual education in school

* *Goal: Make Americans dependent on media*

Outcome: Society reflects the violence of television, film, music, and video games

* *Solution: Gun ban*

Disarm the citizens, continue to glorify violence through the outlets of media

The mentality is simply this, you can kill children all day long, just don't do it with a gun. You can smoke marijuana if you want, as long as we can tax it. You can worship any god you like, just don't display a cross or say, "Merry Christmas." If you oppose abortion or gay marriage, you are a hateful person, but if you support the murder of children and sodomy, you are a peaceful, open-minded individual who is making a positive contribution to the world.

As senseless as it all seems, it will only get much worse before it gets any better. The best preparation that anyone can make is to build a strong relationship with God. Having done this, my wife and I have realized the purpose that God has determined for our lives. And even though we have been shown a glimpse of the horrific things that are soon to come, we have cheerful optimism. Because we know that all things are in God's hand and that we are doing His will.

The Banishment of Evil

When the Antichrist receives his power, he will have achieved the goal of stereotypical evil masterminds that wish to rule the world in the movies. What is more unique about him than any other thing that is written is his punishment. He will be cast alive into the lake of fire. After this, he will spend eternity there. Most would agree that ruling the world for a short number of years would certainly not be worth an eternity in a lake of fire. And yet many will be there, without ever having had the glory of ruling the world.

After the Antichrist is cast into the lake of fire, Satan will be bound for the one thousand-year reign of Christ thus will begin life as it was originally purposed for mankind—a world without the influence of Satan, with a king that has defeated him. Can you imagine the freedom of such safety, the confidence of just laws and decisions, a divine counselor that can be sought face-to-face?

There will be no abominable acts and no one to say, "The devil made me do it!" Aside from the Antichrist being cast alive into the lake of fire and Satan being bound in the bottomless pit, let us take a look at the outcome for all those who followed the beast and did not repent of their sins.

> And the remnant were slain with the
> sword of him that sat upon the horse,
> which sword proceeded out of his
> mouth: and all the fowls were filled
> with their flesh. (Revelation 19:21)

To be counted worthy and not among those who will be banished from this world and the presence of God, we must overcome our sins. And we must also overcome temptation. For it is written:

> He that overcometh shall inherit all things;
> and I will be his God, and he shall be my
> son. But the fearful, and unbelieving, and
> the abominable, and murderers, and
> whoremongers, and sorcerers, and
> idolators, and all liars, shall have their
> part in the lake which burneth with fire
> and brimstone: which is the second death.
> (Revelation 21:7–8)

Just as the world we know will come to an end, we all face our own end on our deathbed. Every day we are closer to our own personal apocalypse. And just as there will be victory in the battle of Armageddon, we must wage our own personal war against evil. We must banish the sin in our own lives.

One huge step toward banishing evil in your own life is to turn off your television. And it is very simple and effective.

Having been a faithful fan of Hollywood blockbusters myself, I made the decision to cut out about 95 percent of the entertainment I was viewing over a year ago. I can assure you, there is no useful information to be gained from years of entertainment. In the one year since I made this decision, I have had the time to more than double my knowledge of the Bible, write three books myself, compose numerous arrangements for classical guitar, and become a successful hunter.

Clearly, this was a positive decision for me as it can be for anyone. Even if I had accomplished little with the free time I have gained, I couldn't go back to watching the screen if I wanted to. It is nearly impossible to view a film, sitcom, or even most commercials today without a Christian bringing vexation upon themselves. This is why it so puzzles me to hear Christians discussing the latest blockbusters that have an R rating due to language that typically takes God's name in vain, violence, gore, and nudity. How can a Christian not choke on their popcorn as they take all of this in?

Take my advice, be a *doer* not a *viewer*. You will not realize how appalling entertainment is today until you see it after a little time without it. You will be amazed that you ever submitted yourself to it at all. The same of course can be said for the genres of the music industry. Our children are given idols to follow that are exceedingly ungodly. In most rock music, there is the influence of drugs, satanic lyrics, and the promotion of rebellion. In rap music, there is the promotion of murder, prostitution, and drug use. In pop music, it is sex and drugs and the encouragement to dress like a whore and wear a pound of make-up or "fake up."

Let us consider the Mozart effect.[9] In the 1950s, Dr. Albert Tomatis achieved success by playing Mozart's work to help people with speech and auditory disorders. In the 1990s, the University of California at Irvine conducted a study that revealed thirty-six students IQ scores went up 8 points after listening to only ten minutes of Mozart. If the theory that classical music can make you smarter is factual, there is no doubt that the genres of today's music can make you dumber. And if you listen to a few of the chart toppers that are repetitively played today, there will be no question as to whether or not they are dumbing down the masses. What is unfortunate for all of us is that these masses are the future of our nation.

King of Kings, Lord of lords

Can you imagine life without the good news of Jesus Christ, without the eradication of our sins and the possibility of redemption? How much worse would the world be if there were no promise of a coming correction? Hope would not exist, and it would all be too unbearable to comprehend. This is the state of hopelessness that will overcome all those who do not seek a covenant with Jesus Christ.

As the age of sin draws to a close, wickedness increases at an unprecedented rate. Why has the world gone crazy, we ask. Because Satan knows that his time is running out. As for the atheists, agnostics, Muslims, and all those who have allowed themselves to be deceived, the world's biggest "I told you so" is coming. For everyone will know the truth as it is written in the following verse.

> That at the name of Jesus every knee should bow, of things in heaven, and things in earth, and things under the earth; And that every tongue should confess that Jesus Christ is Lord, to the glory of God the Father.
> (Philippians 2:10–11)

The world will face unimaginable horror, being subjected to the wrath of Satan, under the rule of the Antichrist. However, it is not such things that we should fear, for we should fear God, who created all things, including even Satan and the Antichrist himself. When Jesus Christ returns as King, he will be most feared of all, for in righteousness he will judge and make war.

Eternal Life, Eternal Light

For those who are accounted worthy, an eternity awaits to be spent in the presence of God. All things will be made new, and there will be no more evil or pain or sorrow. If ever there was an appointment or a destination or a goal to achieve, this is the one you must keep. For many shall not obtain it, though many have considered it. The result of this would be an eternity of sorrow and unimaginable regret. Let us look at the description of the atmosphere that awaits those who have overcome sin.

> And I saw no temple therein: for the Lord God Almighty and the Lamb are the temple of it. And the city had no need of the sun, neither of the moon, to shine in it: for the glory of God did lighten it, and the Lamb is the light thereof. (Revelation 21:22–23)

We know the prize and what we must do to obtain it. We also know the signs of the end and that it is coming fast. Now is the time to be physically, mentally, and most importantly spiritually prepared. For the prophecies of the word of God are about to be made manifest. And as the world begins to tremble, a great deception is in the works. Only those who are not prepared will be deceived.

We know the characteristics of the coming Antichrist and that they are now commonplace in society. It is no longer a question as to whether or not the end is near, but whether or not the end is already here. As the masses are blissfully ignorant of the coming horrors that will soon grip the world, it is ever important to share the testimony of Jesus Christ. I pray that the Lord strengthen those who seek to do his will and may God have mercy. I also pray that if you do not know Jesus Christ personally that you will take the time to know Him and give your life over to His salvation.

Notes

Chapter 2

1. Woman tattoos business ad on forehead for 10,000 dollars

   http://www.deseretnews.com/article/600145187/Mom-sells-face-space-for-tattoo-advertisement.html?pg=all

2. Uprising in Tunisia

   http://www.pbs.org/newshour/rundown/2011/01/state-of-emergency-in-tunisia-amid-mass-protests.html

Chapter 3

1. New Madrid Quakes

   http://en.wikipedia.org/wiki/1812_New_Madrid_earthquake

Chapter 4

1. Obamacare microchip

    http://seniorcitizenspublicsquare.com/2012/11/17/another-hidden-secret-in-obamacare-implanted-microchips/

Chapter 5

1. Invention of the microchip

    http://en.wikipedia.org/wiki/Jack_Kilby

2. High-tech toilet

    http://article.wn.com/view/2010/08/29/Japans_smart_toilet_can_keep_your_health_in_check/

3. Tombstone microchip

    http://www.memorymedallion.com/

4. Verichip

    http://en.wikipedia.org/wiki/VeriChip

5. Nikola Tesla

http://en.wikipedia.org/wiki/Nikola_Tesla

6. Project MKULTRA

http://en.wikipedia.org/wiki/Project_MKUltra

7. 5,000 blackbirds and 100,000 drumfish dead http://www.msnbc.msn.com/id/40887450/ns/us_news-environment/t/fish-found-dead-along-arkansas-river/â˜».UN9N5m873_Q

8. Russian chemtrails

http://www.time.com/time/world/article/0,8599,1930822,00.html

9. Asperatus cloud type

http://en.wikipedia.org/wiki/Asperatus_cloud

10. Henry Kissinger on Obama

http://www.wnd.com/2009/01/85442/

11. Henry Kissinger on America

   http://www.theforbiddenknowledge.com/hardtruth/henry_kissinger.htm

12. Barack Obama on new world order

   http://ivarfjeld.wordpress.com/2011/01/25/obama-all-nations-must-build-global-regime/

13. Al Gore on new world order

   http://www.climatedepot.com/a/1893/Flashback-Gore-US-Climate-Bill-Will-Help-Bring-About-Global-Governance

14. Gordon Brown on new world order

   htt p://edition . cnn . com/2009/WORLD/europe/02/22/germany.financial.summit/index.html

   15. George Bush Sr. on new world order

   http://www.youtube.com/watch?v=Rc7i0wCFf8g

   16. Robert Mueller on new world order

   http://www.arewelivinginthelastdays.com/com/quotes.html

17. Woodrow Wilson on conspiracy

http://www.thirdworldtraveler.com/New_World_Order/WWilson_NewFreedom.html

18. JFK on conspiracy

http://www.youtube.com/watch?v=QeYgLLahHv8

19. Robert Kennedy on new world order

http://www.arewelivinginthelastdays.com/com/quotes.html

20. Georgia Guidestones

http://en.wikipedia.org/wiki/Georgia_Guidestones

Chapter 6

1. Florida zombie attack

http://en.wikipedia.org/wiki/Miami_cannibal_attack

2. Parents murder baby suspected of being demon possessed

http://www.fox19.com/Global/story.asp?s=9457010&clienttype=printable

Chapter 8

1. 1972 Andes plane crash survivors

    http://en.wikipedia.org/wiki/1972_Andes_flight_disaster

2. Side effects of human cannibalism

    http://askville.amazon.com/medical-side-effects-human-cannibalism/AnswerViewer.do?requestId=10668213

3. Suicide statistics

    http://www.cdc.gov/violenceprevention/pdf/suicide_datasheet-a.pdf

4. Drug use statistics

    http://www.samhsa.gov/newsroom/advisories/1109075503.aspx

Chapter 10

1. Nazi concentration camps

    http://en.wikipedia.org/wiki/Nazi_concentration_camps

2. Holocaust data

   http://www.ushmm.org/wlc/en/article.php?moduleId=10005144

   3. Native American detention camps

   http://www.issuesandalibis.org/campsa.html

   4. Rock Island Arsenal

   http://en.wikipedia.org/wiki/Rock_Island_Arsenal

   5. Japanese American internment

   htt p://en . wikipedia . org/wiki/Japanese_American_internment

6. Guantanamo Bay detention camp

   http://en.wikipedia.org/wiki/Guantanamo_Bay_detention_camp

7. Bagram Theatre Internment Facility

   http://en.wikipedia.org/wiki/Detainees_held_in_the_Bagram_Theater_Internment_Facility

8. Abu Ghraib Prison

   http://en.wikipedia.org/wiki/Abu_Ghraib_prison

9. Garden Plot and Rex 84

   http://constitution.org/abus/garden_plot/garden_plot.htm

10. MIAC report

    http://constitution.org/abus/le/miac-strategic-report.pdf

11. DHS assessment

    http://www.ldsresources.net/wp-content/uploads/2009/04/rightwing-dhs.pdf

12. Executive orders

    http://www.disastercenter.com/laworder/12656.htm

Chapter 11

1. The works of Josephus

   The Works of Josephus Complete and unabridged published by; Hendrickson Publishers, Inc. 1991

2. The book of Enoch

   http://www.sacred-texts.com/bib/boe/boe024.htm

   3. New York underground city

   http://en.wikipedia.org/wiki/Underground_city

   4. Chicago Pedway

   http://en.wikipedia.org/wiki/Chicago_Pedway

   5. Denver airport

   http://en.wikipedia.org/wiki/Denver_International_Airport

   6. Phil Schneider underground bases

   http://www.youtube.com/watch?v=Vf7vLXf5bNo

   7. Pope comments on aliens

   http://news.bbc.co.uk/2/hi/7399661.stm

   8. Rumbling noises in Midwest

   http://news.bbc.co.uk/2/hi/7399661.stm

Chapter 13

1. China calls for the disarmament of America

   http://www.infowars.com/communist-chinese-government-calls-for-americans-to-be-disarmed/

   2. Agenda behind women's liberation

   http://www.youtube.com/watch?v=7gwcQjDhZtI

   3. Statistics of divorce rate

   http://www.cdc.gov/nchs/data/vsus/VSUS_1948_1.pdf

4. Statistics of marriage rate

   http://www.cdc.gov/nchs/data/series/sr_21/sr21_016acc.pdf

5. Statistics of non-marital birth rate

   http://www.cdc.gov/nchs/data/vsus/VSUS_1948_1.pdf

6. The Mozart effect

   http://science.howstuffworks.com/environmental/life/inside-the-mind/human-brain/10-brain-myths2.htm

ABOUT THE AUTHOR

Woodrow Polston is the Author of numerous books that are attributed to Biblical studies. Woodrow lives in rural Missouri with his wife, Author Miryah Polston and their three children.

AVAILABLE FROM THE AUTHOR

www.ingramcontent.com/pod-product-compliance
Lightning Source LLC
Chambersburg PA
CBHW061638040426
42446CB00010B/1474